KU-414-018

 bme BUSINESS MANAGEMENT ENGLISH

LANGUAGE REFERENCE FOR BUSINESS ENGLISH

Grammar, functions and communication skills

Nick Brieger
and
Jeremy Comfort

ENGLISH LANGUAGE TEACHING

Prentice Hall International

New York London Toronto Sydney Tokyo Singapore

First published 1992 by
Prentice Hall International
Campus 400, Maylands Avenue
Hemel Hempstead
Hertfordshire HP2 7EZ
A division of
Simon & Schuster International Group

© International Book Distributors Ltd.

All rights reserved. No part of this publication may be
reproduced, stored in a retrieval system, or transmitted,
in any form, or by any means, electronic, mechanical,
photocopying, recording or otherwise, without prior
permission, in writing, from the publisher.
For permission within the United States of America
contact Prentice Hall Inc., Englewood Cliffs, NJ 07632.

Typeset by Keyboard Services, Luton
Printed and bound in Great Britain by Redwood Books, Trowbridge

---

Library of Congress Cataloging-in-Publication Data

Brieger, Nick.
    Language reference for business English / Nick Brieger and Jeremy Comfort
        p.   cm. – (English language teaching) (Business management English)
        Includes index.
        ISBN 0-13-093428-3
        1. English language – Grammar – 1950–   2. English language – Business
    English.   I. Title.   II. Series.   III. Series: Business management
    English series.
        PE1115.B685   1991
    428.2′.2433 – dc20   91–21899
                                                                          CIP

British Library Cataloguing in Publication Data

Brieger, Nick
    Language reference. – (Business management English series)
    I. Title   II. Comfort, Jeremy   III. Series 808

ISBN 0-13-093428-3

---

7 8   98 97 96

Textual overview

LANGUAGE

Part 1   Grammar

Units 1–65

Part 2   Functions

Units 66–82

COMMUNICATION

Skill 1   Presentations

Skill 2   Meetings

Skill 3   Telephoning

Skill 4   Letter-writing

Skill 5   Report-writing

Skill 6   Social language

LANGUAGE REFERENCE FOR BUSINESS ENGLISH

Grammar, functions and
communication skills

BUSINESS MANAGEMENT ENGLISH SERIES

Comfort, J. and N. Brieger
  Marketing
Comfort, J. and N. Brieger
  Finance
Brieger, N. and J. Comfort
  Production and Operations
Brieger, N. and J. Comfort
  Personnel

Other ESP titles of interest include:

Adamson, D.
  Starting English for Business *
Brieger, N. and J. Comfort
  Business Contacts *
Brieger, N. and J. Comfort
  Developing Business Contacts *
Brieger, N. and J. Comfort
  Advanced Business Contacts *
Brieger, N. and A. Cornish
  Secretarial Contacts *
Brieger, N. and J. Comfort
  Technical Contacts *
Brieger, N. and J. Comfort
  Social Contacts *
Brieger, N. and J. Comfort
  Business Issues
Davies, S. *et al.*
  *Bilingual Handbooks of Business
  Correspondence and Communication*
McGovern, J. and J. McGovern
  Bank on Your English *
Palstra, R.
  Telephone English *
Palstra, R.
  Telex English
Pote, M. *et al.*
  A Case for Business English *

* Includes audio cassette(s)

Contents

Sentence and clause types

Nouns

Adjectives and adverbs

Determiners

Part 2   Functions

COMMUNICATION

Introduction

This book is primarily for students – though, of course, it must also be usable by teachers. The students we have in mind as our 'class' are adults who already use English in their studies or their jobs, but need to check it and develop it. This book is, therefore, intended as both a reference book and a practical guide.

In designing this book we have tried to address two concerns of this student group: firstly, the need to develop language knowledge, and secondly, the need to develop communicative skills. We recognise that there are significant overlaps between these two areas, but we believe it is useful to view them separately so that they can be successfully integrated into the total performance. After all, this should be the purpose of language teaching: the total performance that combines accurate language use with effective communicative techniques. The organisation of the material in this book reflects this division. There are two main sections: language and communication.

Turning first to language. Everyone is familiar with the area of language – complex and complete. To use this system accurately, students need to have a good grasp of it. So, we have tried to include most of the core.

Every specialist area has its own specialist terms, and grammar is no exception. We have attempted to keep the jargon to a minimum. However, there are certain conventions we have used which are convenient and simple as short forms. These are:

V1 = the infinitive without **to**
V2 = the past simple form
V3 = the past participle
Am.E. = American English
Br.E. = British English
$\longleftrightarrow$ a time line on which the past lies to the left and the future to the right
present

Vocabulary gives us the words (verbs, nouns and adjectives); grammar gives us the forms to combine these building blocks (sentence and clause patterns, verb tenses and prepositions etc.); and functions enable us to use vocabulary and grammar in order to perform verbally (agreeing, opinion-giving, comparing). Control of the grammar enables us to speak and write accurately; control of the functions enables us to speak and write appropriately in a range of situations.

The final section deals with the total performance. It is divided into six key skills – activities common to all professionals. This section goes beyond the linguistic skills of grammatical accuracy and functional appropriacy. It introduces ideas on techniques and strategies of communication, and presents models on which to build effectiveness for the totally integrated performance.

In trying to achieve completeness as well as variety, much has had to be included in the grammar section to provide the core of the total system; similarly, much has had to be excluded from the section on communication skills because of limitations of space. Any shortcomings in the rest are our responsibility.

Acknowledgements

The authors would like to acknowledge the advice and support of colleagues at York Associates. Thanks are also due to Isobel Fletcher de Téllez for getting the book through its final difficult stages.

The publisher and authors would like to thank the following for their kind permission to reproduce extracts:

Bristol Polytechnic for pages 183, 190, 215 and 227, which are adapted from *Putting It Together*, published by permission of Management Learning Productions, Bristol Polytechnic.
McGraw-Hill for extracts from *How to Communicate* by Gordon Wells (1978).

Every effort has been made to trace and acknowledge ownership of copyright. The publishers will be glad to make suitable arrangements with any copyright holders whom it has not been possible to contact.

LANGUAGE

Part 1
Grammar

UNIT 1
The present continuous

A. *Sample sentences*

- Sales are increasing at the moment.
- At present we are recruiting a new sales director.
- What are you doing? – I am just finishing this report.
- We are starting a new sales campaign next month.

B. *Form*

The present continuous comprises two parts:

the present tense of **to be** + V1 . . . *ing*

1. *Positive form*

I **am checking** the stock.
You/we/they **are checking** . . .
He/she/it **is checking** . . .
We/you/they **are checking** . . .

2. *Negative form*

I **am/'m not expecting** a delivery today . . .
You/we **are not/aren't expecting** . . .
He/she/it **is not/isn't expecting** . . .

3. *Interrogative form*

Am I **getting** the right results?
Are you **getting** . . . ?
Is he/she/it **getting** . . . ?
Are we/you/they **getting** . . . ?

C. *Uses*

We use the present continuous to talk about:

- activities at or around the time of speaking
- temporary activities in the present
- fixed arrangements in the future

1. To indicate an activity at the moment of speaking:
   - What are you doing? – I'm calculating the sales figures.
2. To indicate an activity around the time of speaking:
   - We are installing a new assembly line.

3. To indicate the temporary nature of an activity:
    - I'm working in Paris at the moment. (but normally I work in London)
4. To indicate a fixed arrangement in the future:
    - We are running a training seminar next Monday.

NOTES

1. With C1, 2 and 3, we can use the following time expressions (present time markers):
    at the/this moment
    at present
    currently
    now
2. With C4, we normally use a word or expression to show that we mean future time. This avoids confusion with the present time:
    What are you doing *this evening*? (future)
    cf. What are you doing? (present)

See also
Unit 2 – The present simple
Unit 8 – The future with **will**
Unit 9 – The future with **going to**

UNIT 2
The present simple

A. Sample sentences

- The marketing director reports to the MD.
- We usually hold our European meeting in Madrid.
- I don't understand these statistics.
- My plane leaves at 10.30 on Tuesday.

B. Form

The present simple comprises:

> one part in the positive, i.e. V1(s)
> two parts in the negative and interrogative, i.e. **do/does** + V1

1. Positive form

> I/you/we/they **work** in different departments.
> He/she/it **works** in different departments.

2. Negative form

> I/you/we/they **do not/don't produce** a monthly report.
> He/she/it **does not/doesn't produce** a monthly report.

3. Interrogative form

> **Do** I/you/we/they **need** more information?
> **Does** he/she/it **need** more information?

C. Uses

We use the present simple to talk about:

> - general or permanent activities or situations
> - the frequency of activities
> - truths or current beliefs
> - fixed schedules in the future

1. To indicate a general or permanent activity:
   - The company produces a wide range of pharmaceuticals.
   - I live in Frankfurt.
2. To describe how often an activity is done:
   - We appraise our employees once a year.
3. To describe a truth or current belief:
   - Managers plan, organise, lead and control.

4. To indicate a fixed schedule in the future:
   - The new training programme starts on 1 January.
5. With non-continuous verbs:
   - At present our company belongs to the ABC Group. (*not:* 'is belonging')
   - At the moment the board consists of six people.

The following verbs are usually used only in the simple form:

hope	*know*	*understand*	*like*	*love*	*mean*
forget	*imagine*	*remember*	*prefer*	*suppose*	*want*
belong	*concern*	*consist of*	*contain*	*cost*	*equal*
have	*involve*	*depend on*	*owe*	*possess*	*own*
remain	*require*				

NOTES

1. Remember the **-s** in the third person singular, i.e.

positive	– work**s**
negative	– doe**sn't** work
interrogative	– doe**s** . . . work

2. With C1 and 2, no adverb of time is needed.
3. With C3, we use time expressions to indicate how often something happens. We have two categories of frequency:

   definite frequency
   indefinite frequency

3.1. Indefinite frequency

100%	always
90%	usually/normally
75%	often/frequently
50%	sometimes/occasionally
25%	rarely/seldom
10%	hardly ever
0%	never

The numbers are a general indication, not exact values.

3.2 Definite frequency

every minute		
every hour	or	hourly
every day	or	daily
every week	or	weekly
every month	or	monthly
every year	or	yearly/annually

   once/twice/three times a day/week/month/year

3.3 The position of indefinite frequency markers
   These products *usually* sell for about three years. (before the verb)
   Usually these products sell for about three years. (at the beginning of the sentence)

These products are *usually* in the shops six weeks before Christmas. (after the verb **to be**)

3.4 The position of definite frequency markers

Every year we launch a new model. (at the beginning of the sentence)
We launch a new model *every year*. (at the end of the sentence)

See also
Unit 1 – The present continuous (section C4)
Unit 8 – The future with **will**
Unit 9 – The future with **going to**

UNIT 3
The past simple

A. Sample sentences
- Last year the results were very pleasing.
- During the year we increased sales by 12 per cent.
- In the first quarter the company reduced the workforce by 8 per cent.
- We didn't need to borrow so heavily from the bank.
- When did we reach the breakeven point?

B. Form
The past simple comprises:

> one part in the positive, i.e. V2
> two parts in the negative and interrogative, i.e. **did** + V1

1. Positive form
> Last year I/you/he/she/it/we/they **worked** in personnel.

2. Negative form
> At that time I/you/he/she/it/we/they **did not/didn't know** the forecast.

3. Interrogative form
> **Did** I/you/he/she/it/we/they **fill** in the form correctly?

C. Uses
We use the past simple to talk about activities in the past.
1. To indicate an activity at a specific time in the past:
   - Last week the ABC Group took over our company.
2. To ask when an activity happened:
   - When did the new MD start?

NOTES

1. Once we have explicitly mentioned a specific time in the past, all the following activities are understood to happen within that time frame, i.e. in the past:
   > Last year we appointed a new sales director. After he *took* up his post, he *started* to change the sales regions.

2.   Typical past time markers include:
>   *yesterday*
>   *. . . ago*
>   *last . . .*
>   *on* + day/date,   e.g. on Monday, on 21 January
>   *in* + month/year   e.g. in July, in 1983
>   *at that time*

3.   **Already** and **recently**

In American English **already** is used with the past simple:
>   We already finished the figures.

In British English the present perfect is used (see Unit 5):
>   We have already finished the figures.

Recently is used with both the past simple and the present perfect:
>   I met him recently. (at a specific time in the recent past)
>   I haven't seen him recently. (in the period of time from the recent past till today)

See also
Unit 5 – The present perfect simple

UNIT 4
The past continuous

A. Sample sentences

- Our overseas sales were increasing when our GM resigned.
- While we were waiting for an offer from ABC, a new player came on the scene.
- A. What were you doing at this time last week?
  B. Let me see. Yes, I was just going round the new plant.

B. Form

The past continuous comprises two parts:

the past tense of **to be** + V1 . . . *ing*

1. Positive form

I/he/she/it **was checking** the stock.
You/we/they **were checking** . . .

2. Negative form

I/he/she/it **was not/wasn't expecting** a delivery.
You **were not/weren't expecting** . . .

3. Interrogative form

What **was** I/he/she/it **doing** at this time last year?
What **were** you/we/they **doing** . . . ?

C. Uses

We use the past continuous to provide a past time frame for another activity.
1. Timeframing:
   - Our overseas sales were increasing when the GM resigned.

increase in overseas sales

resignation of GM

The resignation happened at a past point of time (X) within a period.

- What were you doing at this time last year?

What were you doing?

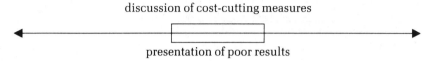

this time last year

This time last year = a past point of time within a time frame; 'what were you doing' indicates a past period of time and provides a time frame for 'this time last year'.

- While we were discussing cost-cutting measures, the GM was presenting the poor results.

discussion of cost-cutting measures

presentation of poor results

Here the time frame 'the GM was presenting the poor results' is not at a point of time (X), but lasts for a period of time (indicated by the lower brace). In fact the two actions happened at the same time and for the same period. Therefore, both verbs are in the past continuous.

NOTES

1. The past continuous does not necessarily mean that an activity lasted for a long time:

   I was working for ABC for ten years. (wrong)
   I worked for ABC for ten years. (right)
   I was working for ABC when the merger took place. (right)

2. Expressions with the preposition **during** can be changed to clauses with **while** + past continuous:

   During the negotiations another offer was made.
   While we were negotiating, another offer was made.
   We didn't say anything during the meeting.
   We didn't say anything while the meeting was going on.

See also
Unit 3 – The past simple

UNIT 5
The present perfect simple

A. Sample sentences

- Have you read the report on rationalisation?
- Turnover has increased by 10 per cent this year.
- The European HQ has been based in Barcelona since 1989.
- Our unpaid debts have now reached an unacceptable level.

B. Form

The present perfect simple comprises two parts:

has/have + V3

1. Positive form

I/you/we/they **have/'ve finished** the project
He/she/it **has/'s finished** the project

2. Negative form

I/you/we/they **have not/haven't** + V3
He/she/it **has not/hasn't** + V3

3. Interrogative form

Have I/you/we/they + V3
Has he/she/it + V3

C. Uses

In meaning, the present perfect simple belongs to the present tenses. This is because in the various uses below, the meaning is always linked to the present rather than the past.

1. To indicate an activity at some non-specific time in the past with an impact or result in the present or future:
    - We have completed the feasibility study. (present result = study is now finished; future impact = we are ready to proceed to the next stage)
    - *cf.* We completed the feasibility study last week. (specific time in the past)
    - We have raised our prices. (present result = higher prices)
    - *cf.* We raised our prices at the beginning of the year. (specific time in the past)
2. To indicate an activity within a period of time which is not yet finished, i.e. unfinished time:
    - Sales have increased this year. (the year is not yet finished)
    - *cf.* Sales increased last year. (last year is finished)

3. To indicate an activity which started in the past and continues to the present:
   - So far/Up to now we have tested three new applications. (in the period between then and now)
   - He has worked as operations manager since 1989. (he started in 1989 and he is still operations manager today)
   - The company has been based here for five years. (it moved here five years ago and is still here today)

NOTES

1. As the activity in C1 happened at a non-specific time in the past, no time marker is used.
2. In C2, typical time markers are:
   > *this morning/week/month/year*
   > *today*
   > *now*

   Just and **just now** are considered as present time markers, so they are used with the present perfect or other present tense:
   > We have just signed the contract.
   > The delivery has just now arrived.

   Recently can also be used with the present perfect (see also Unit 3, Note 3):
   > Recently there have been many changes in the department.

   Already and **yet** both provide a frame of unfinished time; the time frame starts at an unspecified point in the past and continues to the present. **Already** is typically used in positive sentences; **yet** in negative and interrogative sentences:
   > Have you chosen an advertising agency yet? (between then and now)
   > We have already appointed someone for the post. (between then and now)
3. In C3, typical time markers are:
   > *since* (used to indicate the starting point)
   > *for* (used to indicate the period)

   > He has worked in this department since 1989. (starting point)
   > He has worked in this department for five years. (period)

See also
Unit 3 – The past simple
Unit 6 – The present perfect continuous

UNIT 6
The present perfect continuous

A. *Sample sentences*

- A: How long have you been using marketing consultants?
  B: Well, I suppose we've been working with consultants for about three years. We've just started with Stanpath.
  A: Yes, they've been handling the Preston account, haven't they?
  B: Yes, they've established a good name for themselves.

B. *Form*

The present perfect continuous comprises two parts:

the present perfect of **to be** + V1 . . . *ing*

1. *Positive form*

I/you/we/they **have/'ve been using** the agency
He/she/it **has/'s been using** the agency

2. *Negative form*

I/you/we/they **have not been/haven't been** + V1 . . . *ing*
He/she/it **has not been/hasn't been** + V1 . . . *ing*

3. *Interrogative form*

Have I/you/we/they **been** + V1 . . . *ing*
Has he/she/it **been** + V1 . . . *ing*

C. *Uses*

The present perfect continuous belongs to the present tenses because, in its uses, the meaning is always linked to the present rather than the past. We use the present perfect continuous:
1. To indicate an activity at some non-specific time in the past with an impact or result in the present or future:
    - Here's the report. I've been reading it all morning.
Here, the verb phrase 'have been reading the report' indicates an action over a period of time.
    cf. Here's the report. I have finished reading it.
Here, the verb phrase 'have finished reading it' indicates an action at a point of time. 'To finish' cannot happen over a period of time; it indicates an instantaneous action.
    In other words, we use the present perfect continuous with verb phrases which can happen over a period of time; not with verb phrases which happen at a point of time:

- Sales have been falling recently. (right)
- Sales have been stopping falling recently. (wrong)

2. To indicate an activity which started in the past and continues to the present:
    - We have been developing this product for two years.

Again the verb phrase 'have been developing this product' indicates an action over a period of time; in this case the period of time is specified.

Compare the following sentences:
- Since the beginning of the year we have tested three new applications.
- We have been testing three new applications since the beginning of the year.

In the first sentence we are interested in the fact that the tests are now finished and that we can now come to some conclusions, or move on to a new stage in the development cycle. In the second sentence we are interested in the action itself – the testing – and its duration.

See also
Unit 3 – The past simple
Unit 5 – The present perfect simple

UNIT 7
The past perfect

A. Sample sentences

- When the company joined the New York stock market, it had already been on the London market for five years.
- Once the MD had formulated a new direction for the company, he wasted no time in putting it into effect.
- It had been a tough winter. Three senior managers had left the company when John Reed took over.
- The MD reported that the company had had a good year.

B. Form

The past perfect is:

the past of the past simple:

the past of the present perfect:

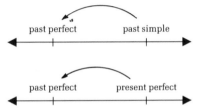

The past perfect comprises two parts:

had + V3

1. Positive form

I/you/he/she/it/we/they **had/'d finished** the project

2. Negative form

I/you/he/she/it/we/they **had not/hadn't** + V3

3. Interrogative form

Had I/you/he/she/it/we/they + V3

C. Uses

We use the past perfect to talk about activities which happened at a time before the past.

1. To indicate an activity at a time before the past:

   - As soon as we had installed the new line, productivity went up.

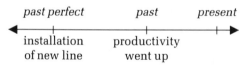

   - Before we installed the new line, productivity had been very low.

2. To report a present perfect tense after a past tense verb of speaking:
   - The MD said, 'We have had a good year.'
   - The MD said that they had had a good year.

   The present perfect in the direct speech in sentence 1 is changed to the past perfect in the indirect speech in sentence 2.

NOTES

1. Often a past simple form is used in place of a past perfect, where the sequence of events is clear:

   > After interest rates rose, many companies went bankrupt. (The use of **after** makes it clear that the first event was the rise in interest rates; therefore the past perfect is not necessary)

2. We use the past perfect with the following time conjunctions:

   after   before   once   until   when   as soon as

See also
Unit 3 – The past simple
Unit 10 – The conditionals
Unit 43 – Clauses of time

UNIT 8
The future with will

A. *Sample sentences*
- In that case I'll collect the goods myself.
- I think I'll go over to the plant and see what the problem is.
- He's gone out. He probably won't be back this afternoon.
- At the next stage, the document will be thoroughly checked.

B. *Form*
The future with **will** comprises two parts:

the modal **will** + V1

1. *Positive form*
I/you/he/she/it/we/they **will/'ll deliver** the goods tomorrow.

2. *Negative form*
I/you/he/she/it/we/they **will not/won't be** at the meeting.

3. *Interrogative form*
Will I/you/he/she/it/we/they **arrive** in time?

C. *Uses*
We use the *modal* **will** to talk about:

- the future
- willingness (see Unit 16)

1. To indicate an activity decided at the time of speaking:
   - A: Have you got last year's figures there?
     B: Sorry no. I'll get them for you now.
     A: It's okay. I won't need them till tomorrow.
     B: Right. I'll ring you back later.
2. To indicate a neutral activity in the future or a part of a process:
   - The meeting will start at 9 o'clock.
   - First I will give a brief account of development during the last six months.
   - At the next stage the subcontractors will send us a detailed account of their findings.
3. After verbs of mental activity, e.g. *think, hope, expect*:
   - I hope the shareholders will accept the new offer.

4. After adverbs of certainty, probability and possibility:
    - Sales will probably fall in the first half of next year as a result of the recession.
5. In the main clause of conditional I sentences:
    - Even if we move into the top end of the market, we won't increase our margins. (*not*: even if we will move . . .)

NOTES

1. The contraction **'ll** can be used after all subjects (noun and pronoun) – but only in speech:
    > The two companies'll merge next month.
2. Future time markers are:
    > *next* . . .
    > *on* + day/date   e.g. on Monday, on 21 January
    > *in* + month/year   e.g. in July, in 1999
3. In C3, the negative of 'I think he will' is usually expressed as 'I don't think he will':
    > I think he will accept our offer.
    > I don't think he will accept our offer. (rather than 'I think he won't accept our offer')

    Notice also:
    > I think so. (positive)
    > I don't think so. (negative)

    Notice, however, the following opposites:
    > I hope/expect he will accept the job
    > I hope/expect he won't accept the job.
4. In C4, notice the word order (**will** and adverb) in the positive and negative sentences:
    > Staff turnover will definitely increase.
    > Staff turnover definitely won't increase.

See also
Unit 1 – The present continuous (section C4)
Unit 2 – The present simple (section C4)
Unit 9 – The future with **going to**
Unit 16 – **Will** and **would**

UNIT 9
The future with going to

A. Sample sentences
- The figures look pretty bad! What are you going to do about them?
- We are going to start the meeting at 9 o'clock.
- I'm going to visit our distributors soon.
- They've just announced a rail strike. That means the delivery is going to be delayed.

B. Form
The future with **going to** consists of three parts:

> **to be** + **going to** + V1

1. Positive form

I am We/you/they **are** He/she/it **is**	**going to**	**check** the details

2. Negative form

I **am not**/**'m not** He/she/it **is not**/**isn't** **He's/she's/it's not** We/you/they **are not**/**aren't** **We're/you're/they're not**	**going to**	**check** the details

3. Interrogative forms

Am I **Is** he/she/it **Are** you/we/they	**going to**	**check** the details?

C. Uses
We use **going to** to talk about activities in the future.
1. To indicate an action that has already been decided:
   - We are going to launch the new model next year.
2. To indicate an intention:
   - What are you going to do this evening?
3. To indicate a future activity based on the present situation:
   - I've just inspected that batch; the customer is certainly not going to accept it.

NOTE

Future time markers are:

> *next* . . .
> *on* + day/date,   e.g. on Monday, on 21 January
> *in* + month/year   e.g. in July, in 1999

See also
Unit 1 – The present continuous
Unit 2 – The present simple
Unit 8 – The future with **will**

UNIT 10
The conditionals

A. Sample sentences

- If we increase production volume, we will benefit from a more economic batch size.
- They can ensure the quality of the product if they train the supervisors.
- We would have to reduce our workforce if the bank refused to extend our credit.
- If the government hadn't introduced the tax incentive scheme, we would have faced serious financial difficulties.
- If a government cuts taxation, it gains a lot of popular support.
- Provided we don't increase expenditure, we will definitely reach break even within six months.

B. Form

A conditional sentence comprises two clauses:

the **if** clause
the main clause

There are four principal types of conditional sentence: conditional I, conditional II, conditional III and universal conditions

Conditional	**If** clause	Main clause
I	present simple	future with **will**
II	past simple	conditional with **would**
III	past perfect	past conditional with **would have**
Universal	present simple	present simple

The following contractions are common in speech:

will – **'ll**, e.g. **I'll**, the company**'ll**
would – **'d**, e.g. they**'d**, it**'d**, the organisation**'d**

One way to remember the forms of conditionals I, II and III is to look at the tense relationships in each column of the figure at the top of page 23.

Look at the **if** clause. The starting point in conditional I is the present; one tense back from the present is the past (conditional II); and one tense back from the past is the past perfect (conditional III).

Now look at the main clause. The starting point is **will** (conditional I); the past of **will** is **would** (conditional II); and the past of **would** is **would have** (conditional III).

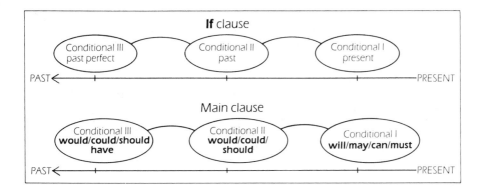

C. Uses

We use conditional sentences to talk about:

— the relationship between events and their consequences:

- If wages rise (event), unemployment will increase (consequence)

As we have seen, there are four principal types of conditional sentence. These reflect the probability of the event and, therefore, its consequence.

1. Conditional I
   Here the speaker sees the event as a real possibility:
   - If we don't install new equipment, we will become uncompetitive.

2. Conditional II
   Here the speaker sees the event as a remote possibility:
   - If we installed the new equipment, we would become more competitive.

3. Conditional III
   Here the speaker recognises that the event is an impossibility, i.e. cannot be fulfilled:
   - If we had installed the equipment, we would have become more competitive. (but we didn't install the equipment; so, we didn't become more competitive)

4. Universal conditions
   Here the speaker indicates that the consequence always follow the event:
   - If the government cuts taxation, it gains a lot of popular support. (increased support is a natural consequence of a cut in taxation)

5. Other conditional markers
   Conditional clauses normally start with **if**. However, the following words and expressions also introduce conditional clauses:

   provided/providing   *on condition that*   *so long as*

   These expressions mean 'if and only if':
   in case   *in the event that*

   These expressions indicate that a future event may or may not happen:
   unless (if not)

   - Provided we don't increase expenditure, we will definitely reach breakeven within six months. (if and only if)

- In case we don't reach the breakeven point within six months, we will have to ask for another bank loan. (we may or may not reach it)
- Unless we reach breakeven point within six months, we will have to ask for another bank loan. (if we don't reach it)

6. Other conditional constructions
    In formal written documents, e.g. legal contracts or agreements, you may find the following conditional constructions:

    Conditional I:
    - Should the agent default on the agreement, we will take legal action.
    should + V1 is an inverted construction in place of 'If the agent defaults'.

    Conditional II:
    - Were the agent to default on the agreement, we would take legal action.
    to be to + V1 in an inverted construction in place of 'If the agent defaulted'.

    Conditional III:
    - Had the agent defaulted on the agreement, we would have taken legal action.
    Inverted past perfect in place of 'If the agent had defaulted'.

NOTES

1. **Will** is a modal verb; in conditional I, other modal verbs can be used in the main clause, e.g. **may** and **must**; similarly in conditionals II and III, the modal in the main clause can be **would** or **might** or **could** or **should**:

    > If our supplier continues to miss deadlines, we must look for alternatives.
    > We might beat the price increases if we made the investments now.
    > If the consultant had done more careful research, he should have identified the gap in the market.

2. There are certain formulae where we can use **would** or **could** after **if**:

    > We would be very grateful/much obliged if you would/could send us the information as soon as possible.

See also
Unit 16 – **Will** and **would**
Unit 18 – **Can** and **could**
Unit 20 – **Shall** and **should**

UNIT 11
Tense review

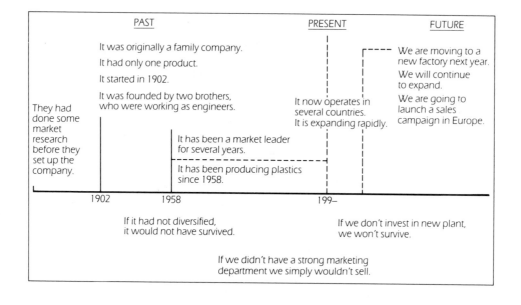

PAST · PRESENT · FUTURE

It was originally a family company.

It had only one product.

It started in 1902.

It was founded by two brothers, who were working as engineers.

They had done some market research before they set up the company.

It now operates in several countries.
It is expanding rapidly.

We are moving to a new factory next year.
We will continue to expand.
We are going to launch a sales campaign in Europe.

It has been a market leader for several years.

It has been producing plastics since 1958.

1902   1958   199–

If it had not diversified, it would not have survived.

If we don't invest in new plant, we won't survive.

If we didn't have a strong marketing department we simply wouldn't sell.

UNIT 12
Verb . . . ing

A. Sample sentences

- He is responsible for checking the stock level in the warehouse.
- They have succeeded in entering a very competitive market.
- They finished testing the prototype two weeks ago.
- Placing an advertisement in a national newspaper attracts less interest than using a specialist journal.
- Is it really worth spending so much money on this project?

B. Form

The verb . . . *ing* form comprises:

> V1 . . . *ing*

It can be seen in:

- the present continuous verb, e.g. I **am going**
- adjective forms, e.g. an **interesting** product
- the present participle, e.g. I heard the MD **presenting** the results
- noun forms, e.g. interested in **increasing** our market share

C. Uses

In noun forms, the verb . . . *ing* functions as a noun and can be called a verbal noun, i.e. a noun made from a verb. It is also called a *gerund*. We use it:

- as the subject or object of a verb
- after a preposition

1. As the subject of a verb:
    - Controlling the company's finances is very important for the health of the organisation.
      - *cf.* He has a controlling interest in the company. (here 'controlling' is an adjective)
    - Brainstorming can help us reach a decision.

2. As the object of a verb:
    Certain verbs must be followed by a verb . . . *ing* (and not an infinitive)
    - We avoided losing the contract by reducing our offer price.
    - I suggested meeting again after we had all read the proposals.

These verbs include:

acknowledge	*dislike*	*miss*	*risk*
avoid	*enjoy*	*postpone*	*stop*
consider	*finish*	*practise* (Br.E)	*suggest*
delay	*involve*	*practice* (Am.E.)	
deny	*don't/doesn't mind*	*regret*	

3. After a preposition:
   Prepositions are always followed by nouns
   - After looking at your products we would like to discuss prices.
   - We look forward to meeting you.

4. After certain phrases:
   (not) worth   *have trouble/difficulty*   *spend/waste time*

   - Is it really worth spending so much money on this project?
   - Workers sometimes have trouble remembering simple details.
   - Not all salesmen should spend time looking for new clients.

NOTE

To can be either a preposition or a particle, i.e.:
   We are used to paying high prices. (preposition followed by verb . . . *ing*)
   We used to buy from a local supplier. (particle followed by infinitive)

See also
Unit 13 – Infinitive
Unit 14 – Verb . . . *ing* or infinitive + **to**

UNIT 13
Infinitive

A. Sample sentences

- The employees agreed to accept the terms of the pay deal.
- At the last moment they decided not to continue with the negotiations.
- The management seem to be moving in the right direction.
- The two sides appear to have solved the problem.
- It is important to carry out these changes as quickly as possible.
- To encourage our employees to develop their skills is one of the prime concerns of management.

B. Form

There are three infinitive forms:

the *present simple infinitive*　　– V1
the *present continuous infinitive* – **to be** + V1 . . . *ing*
the *present perfect infinitive*　　– **to have** + V3

We distinguish between the infinitive with **to** and the 'bare infinitive' without **to** (see Note 1).

C. Uses

We use the infinitive:

- – as the subject or object of a verb
- – after an adjective

1.　As the subject of a verb:
   - To enter this market requires a lot of hard work.
2.　As the object of a verb:
   - We have decided not to advertise this position, but to recruit internally.
3.　After an adjective:
   - I am glad to inform you that you have been successful.
   - It is impossible for us to accept these terms.
4.　The tenses
　　We normally use the present simple infinitive to link two verbs:
   - We would like to extend our overdraft facilities.

We use the present continuous infinitive to highlight that the action is happening at the time of speaking:
   - The management seem to be moving in the right direction. (it seems that they are moving in the right direction)

We use the present perfect infinitive to highlight that the action of the infinitive happened before the action of the first verb:

- The two sides appear to have solved the problem. (it appears that the two sides have solved the problem)
- The sales director claimed to have found three new customers. (the sales director claimed that he had found three new customers)

NOTES

1. The particle **to** is needed to link a full verb with an infinitive; the bare infinitive is used after modals:

can/could   may/might   shall/should
will/would   must   needn't

Two exceptions are *help* and *dare* (both full verbs) which can take an infinitive with **to** or a bare infinitive:

Wage increases have helped (to) push up prices.
After the acquisition they didn't dare (to) replace the whole management team immediately.

2. In adjective + infinitive constructions, notice the use of the preposition **for**:
It is important for you to review the candidates.

3. Notice the form of the negative infinitive:
We are glad not to announce a fall in profits.
They promised not to infringe copyright.

See also
Unit 12 – Verb . . . *ing*
Unit 14 – Verb . . . *ing* or infinitive + **to**

UNIT 14
Verb . . . ing or infinitive + to

A. Sample sentences

- We would like to start production as soon as possible.
- We like receiving visitors from our European HQ.
- We like to complete the forecasts for the following year by the beginning of November.
- We are trying to establish a joint venture with a South American company.
- We have already tried working with a number of agents in the Far East.
- They started manufacturing in Hong Kong two years ago.
- They started to manufacture in Hong Kong two years ago.

B. Form

The verb phrase comprises two verbs. The second verb is:

a verb . . . *ing* or an infinitive

C. Uses

1. The meaning of the first verb is different depending on the construction:
    - We stopped producing the A32 last year. (we stopped the production)
    - We stopped to produce the A33. (we stopped the production of something else in order to produce the A33)
2. The meaning of the verb changes slightly with the construction:
    - We like receiving visitors from our European HQ. (we enjoy it)
    - We like to complete the forecasts for the following year by the beginning of November. (it is a good thing to do)
    - We would like to start production as soon as possible. (it is our present desire, i.e. we want)

Other verbs are:

remember
- We remembered to notify our clients in time. (didn't forget)
- I remember receiving a brochure from your company. (I received it and I remember that I did)

try
- We are trying to establish a joint venture with a South American company. (attempting)
- We have already tried working with a number of agents in the Far East. (experimented)

like (see C1 above)

3. There is no systematic difference in meaning:
    - They started manufacturing in Hong Kong two years ago.
    - They started to manufacture in Hong Kong two years ago.

    Other verbs are:

    begin   *continue*   *intend*   *love*   *prefer*   *hate*

See also
Unit 12 – Verb . . . *ing*
Unit 13 – Infinitive

UNIT 15
Verb + object + infinitive

A. *Sample sentences*
- We have asked our customers to settle their invoices within 30 days.
- Our European HQ have invited us to suggest alternative schemes.
- The new policy doesn't let us make enough decisions ourselves. In fact, it makes us rely too much on the line managers.

B. *Form*
The object + infinitive form comprises:

noun or pronoun + infinitive

C. *Uses*
1. Verbs which are always followed by an infinitive with **to**:
    - We want to introduce the changes as soon as possible.
    - We want them to introduce the changes as soon as possible. (*not:* We want that they introduce the changes as soon as possible.)

    Other verbs are:

    ask   expect   would like   would prefer

2. Verbs which are followed by verb . . . *ing* or an object + infinitive:
    - The trade union recommended increasing the annual bonus. (*not:* The trade union recommended to increase the annual bonus.)
    - The trade union recommended the workers to accept the offer.

    Other verbs are:

    allow   permit   advise   encourage

3. Verbs which only take an object + infinitive:
    - The chairman told them not to accept the offer. (*not:* The chairman told not to accept the offer.)

    Other verbs are:

    enable   persuade   order   warn   invite

    - The new system will enable us to process orders more quickly.
4. Verbs which take an object + bare infinitive (without **to**):

    The new personnel policy lets us take initiatives.

    Other verbs are:

    make   help

    - Could you help me (to) translate this document?

NOTES

1. Compare the following sentences:

    He told them to reduce costs.

    He said (to them) that they should reduce costs. (*not:* takes an object + infinitive)

    Tell takes an object + infinitive; *say* takes an indirect object (optional) + clause

2. *Expect* can be followed by an infinitive or a clause:

    We expect interest rates to rise next week.

    We expect that interest rates will rise next week.

See also

Unit 12 – Verb . . . *ing*

Unit 13 – Infinitive

Unit 14 – Verb . . . *ing* or infinitive + **to**

UNIT 16
Will *and* would

A. Sample sentences
- I'll pick you up at your hotel at 9 o'clock.
- I tried to persuade them, but they wouldn't accept the offer.
- Would you ask the next candidate to come in please?
- A: I haven't got the figures here.
  B: Okay, will you please circulate them before the next meeting?

B. Form
Will and **would** are *modals*. **Would** is the past tense form of **will**. Both verbs take a bare infinitive (V1).
The contracted forms are **'ll** and **'d**.
The negative forms are **will not/would not**; the contracted forms are **won't/wouldn't**.

C. Uses
We use **will** and **would** to talk about willingness
1. In requests for action or information:
   - Will you arrange a taxi for me, please? (Are you willing to arrange a taxi for me, please?)
   - Would you ask John to come in, please?
   - Will you tell us if the MD has accepted our proposal?

   The past tense form **would** is more remote (in time) and, therefore, less direct and more polite.
2. In replies to requests:
   - A: Will you arrange a taxi for me, please?
     B: Yes, of course I will. For what time? (yes, of course I am willing to)
3. In offers:
   - I'll have the report ready by tomorrow morning. (I offer to have the report ready by tomorrow morning)
4. Willingness and refusal:
   - A: How did the negotiations go?
     B: Quite well. They will accept our price. (they are willing to accept our price)
     A: And the payment terms?
     B: No, I'm afraid they wouldn't accept the 30-day clause. (they refused to accept the 30-day clause)

NOTES

1. In C1, **will** and **would** are only used in requests with the subject **you**.
2. In C2, we can use different subjects:

> A: Will you arrange a taxi for me, please?
> B: Either I will or one of my colleagues will.

See also

Unit   8 – The future with **will**
Unit 10 – The conditionals
Unit 82 – Requesting information and action

UNIT 17
May *and* might

A. Sample sentences

- We are having a good year and sales may exceed our forecast by 15 per cent.
- Because of the good results, we might bring the investment forward.
- May I interrupt the discussion to report the latest news?
- This is a danger area. Employees may not enter this area without protective clothing.
- A: There seems to be something wrong with the accounts.
  B: Yes, I think the auditors might have overlooked the interest payments we received.
- Might I suggest that we postpone this matter till later.

B. Form

May and **might** are modals. **Might** is the past tense form of **may**. Both verbs take a bare infinitive (V1).

The negative forms are **may not/might not**. The contracted form of **might not** is **mightn't**.

C. Uses

We use **may** and **might** to talk about:

- possibility
- permission

1. Present possibility:
  - A: Can I speak to Peter Franks, please?
    B: Yes, I think he may be back from lunch now.
  - *or* B: Yes, I think he might be back from lunch now. (it is possible that he is back from lunch now)

Both **may** and **might** express present possibility. **May** expresses stronger possibility than **might**:
  - A: Can I speak to Peter Franks, please. He was in a meeting before.
    B: Just one moment. I think the meeting may/might have finished now. (it is possible that the meeting has finished now)

2. Future possibility
   Both **may** and **might** express future possibility. **May** expresses stronger possibility than **might**.
   - Next year we may/might launch a sales campaign in Japan. (it is possible that next year we will launch a sales campaign in Japan)
   - By this time next year we may/might have completed our forecasts. (it is possible that by this time next year we will have completed our forecasts)
   - If we replace our present agent, we may/might still reach target sales. (it is still possible that we will reach target sales)
3. Requests for permission:
   - May/might I make a comment at this point? (is it permitted for me to make a comment at this point?)
   The past tense form **might** is more remote (in time) and, therefore, less direct and more polite.
4. Permission and prohibition:
   - A: May/might I make a comment at this point?
     B: Yes, of course you may. (*not:* of course you might) (it is permitted for you to make a comment)
   - This is a danger area. Employees may not enter this area without protective clothing. (*not:* employees might not) (employees are not permitted to enter this area without protective clothing)

NOTES

1. In C3, **may** and **might** are only used in requests with the subject **I**.
2. In C4, we can use different subjects:
   A: May/might I make a comment at this point?
   B: Yes, of course you may or Dr Jones may.
3. Normally we use **may** rather than **might** to indicate permission and prohibition. However, in indirect speech we can use **might** after a past tense verb of speaking:
   The MD said that employees might participate in the share ownership scheme.
   This sentence has two possible interpretations:
   (i) The MD said that employees were permitted to participate in the scheme.
   (ii) The MD said that it was possible for employees to participate in the scheme.

See also
Unit 18 – **Can** and **could**
Unit 19 – **Must, mustn't** and **needn't**
Unit 80 – Scale of likelihood

UNIT 18
Can *and* could

A. *Sample sentences*

- Our new bottling machine can fill 1,000 bottles per hour.
- When I worked for ABC Group, only the purchasing manager could authorise the purchase of office equipment.
- It's a company rule – personnel can't smoke in the company canteen.
- A: Can I help you?
  B: Yes, can I speak to Paul Griffiths, please?
  A: I'm afraid you can't. He's in a meeting at the moment.
- If we don't deliver today, we can certainly deliver tomorrow.

B. *Form*

Can and **could** are modals. **Could** is the past tense form of **can**. Both verbs take a bare infinitive (V+1).
The negative forms are **cannot/could not**; the contracted forms are **can't** and **couldn't**.

C. *Uses*

We use **can** and **could** to talk about:

- ability
- possibility
- permission

1. Ability:
   - We can certainly review the manning levels in this meeting. (present ability: we are able to review the manning levels in this meeting)
   - Next year, after Peter Barnes finishes his training programme, he can take over the control function. (future ability: he will be able to take over the control function)
   - When I was area manager, I could visit five customers a day. (past ability: I was able to visit five customers a day)

2. Possibility
   Both **can** and **could** express present and future possibility. **Can** expresses stronger possibility than **could**:
   - The components arrived three weeks late. It wasn't their fault. Those problems can/could happen to anybody. (present possibility: it is possible that those problems happen to anybody)
   - We have no idea what can/could happen to their next delivery. (future possibility)

- They sent the goods two weeks ago; so, they could have arrived by now. (*not:* they can have arrived) (present possibility in relation to earlier action: it is possible that they have arrived by now)
- There was no delivery yesterday; so they can't/couldn't have arrived then. (present impossibility in relation to earlier action: it is impossible that they arrived yesterday)

3. Permission:
    - Only employees can buy produce from the company shop. (present permission: only employees are permitted to buy)
    - When I worked there, only supervisory staff could buy produce from the company shop. (past permission: only supervisory staff were permitted to buy)
    - It's a company rule – personnel can't smoke in the company canteen. (present prohibition: personnel are not permitted to smoke in the company canteen)
    - When I worked there, personnel couldn't smoke anywhere in the compound. (past prohibition: personnel were not permitted to smoke in the compound)

NOTES

1. Sometimes it is difficult to distinguish between ability and possibility. This can lead to misunderstanding.

    The MD can be late. (he is able – because of his position; it is possible that he will be – because of other circumstances)

    As the **can** of possibility has the same meaning as the **may** of possibility, we can use **may** to avoid any possible ambiguity.

    They can deliver on time (they are able to)

    They may deliver on time (it is possible that they will)

2. In C1, we can use **can** to indicate future ability; if we want to emphasise the ability we can use **will be able to**.

3. We don't use **can** + present perfect infinitive:

    He could have finished the work by now (*not:* he can have finished the work by now)

    cf. He can't/couldn't have finished the work by now. (both forms possible)

See also
Unit 17 – **May** and **might**
Unit 19 – **Must**, **mustn't** and **needn't**
Unit 79 – Ability and inability

UNIT 19
Must, mustn't *and* needn't

A. Sample sentences

- All shareholders must receive an invitation to the AGM; however, they needn't attend.
- We sent out the invitations a week ago; they must have arrived by now.
- The regulations are quite clear; we must accept a proposal with an absolute majority; we mustn't reject a proposal without presenting it to the meeting.

B. Form

Must, **mustn't** and **needn't** are modals. They take a bare infinitive (V1).
We use the negatives **must not** and **need not** in writing and speech; we generally use the contracted forms **mustn't** and **needn't** only in speech.
The positive of **needn't** is **need**. **Need** is a full verb and takes an infinitive + **to** (see Note 4).

C. Uses

We use **must**, **mustn't** and **needn't** to talk about:

    – necessity to do something (obligation)
    – necessity not to do something (prohibition)
    – logical deduction

1. Necessity to do something (obligation):
   - All invoices must be paid not later than 30 days from date of issue. (it is necessary that all invoices are paid)
2. Necessity not to do something (prohibition):
   - This suggestion from the quality circle is unrealistic; however, we mustn't reject it without discussing it with them. (it is necessary not to reject it)
3. No necessity to do something:
   - If there isn't time, we can look at this matter at our next meeting. It isn't urgent; we needn't discuss it today. (it is not necessary to discuss it today)
4. Logical deduction:
   - A: We have reduced overheads by 25 per cent; these figures can't be right. There must be a mistake somewhere. (it is a logical deduction – from the reduced overheads – that there is a mistake in the figures)
     B: Yes, I agree, but it needn't be in this column here. (it is not a logical deduction that it is in this column)
   - We sent out the invitations a week ago; they must have arrived by now. (it is a logical deduction that they have arrived by now)

NOTES

1. The past of **must** (obligation) is **had to**; the past of **must** (logical deduction) is **must have**
   + V3:

   > He had to make a decision yesterday. (it was necessary to make the decision
   > yesterday)
   > He must have made a decision yesterday. (it is a logical deduction that he made
   > the decision yesterday)

2. The past of **mustn't** (prohibition) is **were not allowed/permitted to**:

   > For reasons of confidentiality we were not allowed to give details to the press.

3. **Mustn't** (prohibition), **can't** (no permission), and **may not** (no permission) have similar
   meanings:

   > In the new flexitime system, employees mustn't/can't/may not take less than
   > half an hour for lunch.

4. The positive of the modal **needn't** is the full verb **need**. **Need** is followed by an infinitive
   + to:

   > We need to finish this meeting by 12 o'clock.

   In the negative, we have two possible constructions:

   > We don't need to finish this meeting before 12 o'clock.
   > We needn't finish this meeting before 12 o'clock.

   The past of **need** is **needed**; the past of **needn't** is **didn't need**.
   Both are followed by an infinitive **+ to**:

   > We needed to replace this piece of equipment.
   > We didn't need to replace this piece of equipment.

See also

Unit 17 – **May** and **might**
Unit 18 – **Can** and **could**
Unit 78 – Obligations and requirements

UNIT 20
Shall *and* should

A. *Sample sentences*
- Shall I present the end-of-year figures now?
- Should we tell him the bad news now?
- You should receive confirmation within the next few days.
- Sales should peak around the middle of next year.
- Both parties shall be bound by the arbitration clause.
- If you want my advice, you should find another supplier.
- Should you require any further information, don't hesitate to contact me.

B. *Form*
Shall and **should** are modals. Both verbs take a bare infinitive (V1).
The negative forms are **shall not** and **should not**; the contracted forms are **shan't** and **shouldn't**.

C. *Uses*
We use **shall** and **should** to:

- talk about the future
- make suggestions
- give advice
- express probability
- express obligation
- express a condition

1. The future
    After **I** and **we**, we can use **shall** in place of **will**:
    - First we shall review last year's figures.
2. Making suggestions
    We use **shall** and **should** followed by **I** or **we** in the question form:
    - Shall we start the meeting?
    - I think we've covered that point in great detail. Should I move on to the next item now?
    The past tense form **should** is more remote (in time) and, therefore, less direct and more polite.
3. We use **should** to give advice:
    - If you want my advice, you should find another supplier. (it would be a good idea to find another supplier)
    - The company shouldn't waste any more time on this project. (it would not be a good idea to waste any more time)

4. We use **should** to express probability:
    - A: Can I speak to Peter Franks, please?
      B: Yes, I think he should be back from lunch now. (present probability: it is probable that he is back now)
    - Sales should reach their peak by the middle of next year. (future probability: it is probable that sales will reach their peak)
    - They sent the goods two weeks ago; so, they should have arrived by now. (present probability in relation to earlier action: it is probable that they have arrived by now)
5. We use **shall** to express obligation, particularly in official orders and legal documents:
    - The supplier shall deliver the goods FOB. (the supplier must deliver the goods FOB)
    - Personnel shall not enter the computer room without the permission of the senior operator. (personnel must not enter the computer room)
6. Expressing a condition
    We can use an inverted construction with **should** in conditional I:
    - Should you require any further information, please contact me. (if you require any further information, please contact me)
    The construction with **should** is rather formal. We use it in official letters and documents.

See also
Unit 10 – The conditionals
Unit 16 – **Will** and **would**
Unit 19 – **Must**, **mustn't** and **needn't**
Unit 81 – Advising and suggesting

UNIT 21
Active

A. *Sample sentences*

- The company manufactures a wide range of electronic components.
- The company started to produce components twelve years ago.
- Next year we will expand into two overseas markets.
- If the market for our products expands, we will have a 20 per cent increase in turnover next year.
- We have been discussing the possibility of collaboration with three European companies.
- The human resources director has said that he would like to introduce a new working system.

B. *Form*

The active sentence contains:

> a subject
> an active verb form

The subject normally comes before the verb:
> The company makes electronic parts.

The active verb is *transitive* or *intransitive*. A transitive verb is followed by a direct object, i.e. the object comes after the verb:
> The company **manufactures** a wide range of electronic components. (object: a wide range of electronic components)
> They hope to expand. (object: to expand)
> We enjoyed visiting your plant. (object: verb . . . *ing*)
> The human resources director **has said** that he would like to introduce a new working system. (object: that he would like to introduce a new working system)

An intransitive verb is not followed by a direct object:
> Next year we **will expand** into two overseas markets. (into two overseas markets = prepositional phrase)
> The market for our products **is expanding**.

The active verb form can be:

> a full verb:
> > We **are investigating** the market now.
> an infinitive:
> > We hope **to enter** the market next year.
> verb . . . *ing*:
> > We enjoyed **seeing** the range of products.

The active verb forms can be in different tenses:

full verbs (see Units 1, 2, 3, 5, 7)
infinitives (see Unit 13)
verb . . . *ing* (see Unit 12)

C. Uses

We use the active form in both spoken and written language to describe events and activities.

We use the passive form in spoken and written language to achieve a specific effect (see Unit 22).

In general, the active creates a more personal effect:

- First we prepare a job description. (here 'we' can mean the speaker and the listeners or simply 'one' – an unidentified person)

   cf.   First a job description is prepared.

NOTES

1.   The normal word order in active sentences is:

Subject	Verb	Object	Rest of sentence
We	opened	the factory	two months early in March

2.   We use an active subject construction after *happen*, *arise* and *occur*

An explosion happened at the plant. (*not*: it happened an explosion at the plant)

A problem arose during the installation. (*not*: it arose a problem during the installation)

See also
Unit 22 – Passive

UNIT 22
Passive

A. Sample sentences

- This question was raised at the last meeting. And no conclusion was reached then.
- At the first stage the raw materials are loaded into this container.
- A: ABC seem to have changed their strategy. Now they want their products to be included in the next catalogue.
  B: Well, they could be successful by being seen in the right company.

B. Form

	Simple	Continuous
Present	they **are developed** **to be** (present) + V3	they **are being developed** **to be** (present) + **being** + V3
Past	they **were developed** **to be** (past) + V3	they **were being developed** **to be** (past) + **being** + V3
Present perfect	they **have been developed** **to be** (present perfect) + V3	Ø
Past perfect	they **had been developed** **to be** (past perfect) + V3)	Ø
Present infinitive	**to be developed** **to be** + V3	**to be being developed** **to be** + **being** + V3
Present perfect infinitive	**to have been developed** **to be** (present perfect) + V3	Ø

C. Uses

We use the passive:

- to avoid mentioning the doer
- to emphasise the doer
- in process descriptions
- in impersonal language

1. Avoiding mentioning the doer:
    - A personnel manager has now been appointed.
    We are not interested in who made the appointment; so an active sentence can't be used.

---

2. Emphasising the doer:
   - These products have been designed by a special team.

   In speech, we usually put the information to be emphasised at the end of a clause. We call this 'end-weight'. So here 'special team' gets more focus than 'these products'.
3. In process descriptions:
   - At the first stage the raw materials are loaded into this container.

   We are not interested in the doer but in the action.
4. In impersonal language:
   - Protective clothing must be worn at all times.

   The passive is widely used in formal written announcements, where an impersonal tone is intended.

See also
Unit 21 – Active

UNIT 23
Be

A. Sample sentences

- We are very interested in seeing your new product range.
- Have you ever been to Japan before?
- They are moving their offices to the new industrial estate.
- The managing director is to make a statement tomorrow about the current financial crisis.

B. Form

| | Positive | Negative | |
		Uncontracted	Contracted
Present			
I	am/'m	am not	(aren't)/'m not
You/we/they	are/'re	are not	aren't/'re not
He/she/it	is/'s	is not	isn't/'s not
Past (V2)			
I	was	was not	wasn't
You/we/they	were	were not	weren't
He/she/it	was	was not	wasn't
V1 . . . ing	being	not being	
V3	been	not been	

NOTES

1. We use **aren't I** as the contracted negative in questions, e.g.:
    > I'm visiting our plant in Spain next week, **aren't I**?
    However, there is no parallel contracted form for positive sentences.
2. In negative commands, we use the modal **don't**, e.g.:
    > Let me give you some advice. **Don't** be late for the meeting.

C. Uses

We use **be**:

- as a full verb
- as an auxiliary verb
- in the construction **be to**

1. Full verb:
   - We are very interested in seeing your new product range.
2. Auxiliary verb:
   We use **be** in the continuous verb forms, e.g.:
   - We are coming to the end of our trading year.
   and in the passive verb froms, e.g.:
   - The productivity bonus was introduced last year.
3. The construction **be to**
   Indicating what must or must not happen:
   - The contract is not to be signed before we have checked that all the parts have been delivered.
   Indicating what should happen:
   - What time am I to come for the appraisal interview?
   Indicating what is going to happen:
   - The managing director is to make a statement tomorrow about the current financial crisis.
   Indicating what cannot or could not happen:
   - The factory is completely empty. There's no-one to be seen.
4. **It is** versus **there is**
   Compare the following sentences:
   - Our existing equipment needs replacement. It is time to invest in new equipment. (now)
   - Don't worry. There is time to change the figures before the meeting. (enough time)
   '*It is time* to do something' means 'we must do it now'; '*there is time* to do something' means 'there is still enough time to do it'. Now compare the following sentences:
   - A: Have you visited their head office?
     B: Yes, it's in New York now, isn't it? (the head office)

   - A: Do you know their management structure?
     B: Not really.
     A: Well, there is an MD supported by a finance manager and a marketing manager. (there exists an MD, etc.)

   - A: George is leaving, you know?
     B: Yes, I've heard. The problem is that it is not easy to replace him as he has a rare combination of skills and knowledge. (to replace him is difficult)

   In the first exchange **it** refers to information that has already been identified, i.e. the head office. In the second exchange **there** introduces new information – the introductory **there**. The word **there** has no specific meaning: it indicates that the key information will follow, i.e. the management structure that B doesn't know.

   cf. A: Do you know their management structure?
   B: Yes, it's quite simple, isn't it . (B already knows 'it')

   In the third exchange the **it** is an 'empty **it**', which is an uncommon construction. In order to give more emphasis to this information we need to put **it** at the end of the sentence (see Unit 22, C2), resulting in the 'empty **it**' construction. The meaning is 'to replace him is difficult'. This construction is uncommon. In any case, information at the end of a sentence carries more emphasis.

NOTES

1. We use an adjective after **be**, not an adverb:

    It is normal to appoint agents for an initial period of one year.

2. We use **be** in the continuous form when we want to emphasise the verb's activity meaning:

    The subcontractors say they can't finish the work until the end of March. I don't understand why they are being so difficult. (they are behaving)

3. **There** can be followed by a singular or plural verb. The verb form depends on the subject of the sentence:

    There is a restaurant in Manila where you can eat excellent seafood.

    There are four tasks associated with management – planning, leading, organising and controlling.

See also

Unit   1 – The present continuous
Unit   4 – The past continuous
Unit   6 – The present perfect continuous
Unit 22 – Passive
Unit 48 – Adjectives versus adverbs

UNIT 24
Verbs of speaking: say, tell, talk, speak *and* discuss

A. *Sample sentences*

- They said that the agreement would be completed by the end of June.
- This morning I would like to tell you a little about the operation of our computer system.
- A: Have you talked to Jim about the forthcoming European meeting?
  B: Yes, I spoke to him about it yesterday. He said he can't make it.
  A: Well, never mind. So, when can we discuss the presentation that we are going to make?
  B: Whenever suits you.

B. *Form*

V1	V2	V3
say	said	said
tell	told	told
talk	talked	talked
speak	spoke	spoken
discuss	discussed	discussed

C. *Uses*

Say

- They said (to us) that the agreement would be completed by the end of June.

To say (to someone) that:

not: They said us that the agreement would be completed.

Tell

- This morning I would like to tell you a little about the operation of our computer system.
- He told us that the system was working well.
- I told him to come as soon as he could

To tell someone that
To tell someone to do something
To tell someone something

not: I would like to tell about our new system.
nor: I would like to tell to you about our new system.

Talk

- Have you talked to Jim about the forthcoming European meeting?

To talk (to someone) about something (Br.E)
To talk (to/with someone) about something (Am.E.)
Talk applies to a whole conversation.
Talk is not a reporting verb
    not: He talked that he would like to see me.

Speak

- I spoke to him about the meeting yesterday.

To speak (to/with someone) about something
Speak applies to a whole conversation or just a part of it.

- Can I speak to Mr Jones, please? (on the telephone)
    not: Can I talk to Mr Jones, please?

Speak is not a reporting verb
    not: He spoke that he would like to visit the plant.

Discuss

- When can we discuss the presentation that we are going to make?

Discuss something (with someone)
    not: When can we discuss about the presentation?

See also
Unit 25 – Verbs of reporting

UNIT 25
Verbs of reporting

A. Sample sentences

- The chairman reported that the companies' performance had been very good.
- He promised that there would be a good dividend on shares this year.
- However, he warned us not to be too optimistic about the medium-term future.

B. Form

Verbs of reporting can take different constructions. Below is the range of constructions and a range of verbs.

	say	present	ask	admit
object (1)		✓	✓	✓
infinitive + **to** (2)			✓	
that + clause (3)	✓			✓
verb . . . *ing* (4)				✓
object + infinitive + **to** (5)			✓	

Here are some sample sentences which show the use of these verbs:

He said **that they had incurred substantial losses.**   (3)
Then he presented **the figures.**   (1)
He asked **to address** the meeting.   (2)
He asked **them to report back** to the next meeting.   (5)
He admitted **all the charges** against him.   (1)
He admitted **that the company was in a bad financial situation.**   (3)
He admitted **receiving** the report a week earlier.   (4)

C. Uses

Below are some of the more common verbs of reporting, classified according to constructions 1–5 in the table above.

1. These verbs only take an object (type 1):

    describe   outline   present

2. These verbs take an infinitive + **to** (type 2); if they take any other constructions as well, they are shown in brackets:

    agree (3)   claim (3)   consent   decline (1)
    demand (1, 3)   promise (1, 3)   propose (1, 3)   refuse (1)
    swear (3)   threaten (1, 3)

3. These verbs take **that** + clause (type 3); if they take any other constructions as well, they are shown in brackets:

announce (1)	assume	believe (1)	confirm (1)
consider (1)	declare (1)	demonstrate (1)	disclose (1)
estimate (1)	explain (1)	guess (1)	hold
indicate (1)	inform	maintain (1)	notify (1)
presume	prove (1)	report (1)	say
show (1)	state (1)		

4. These verbs take an verb . . . *ing* (type 4); if they take any other constructions as well, they are shown in brackets:

admit (1, 5)	advise (1, 5)	authorise (1, 5)	recommend (1, 5)
require (1, 5)	suggest (1, 5)	urge (1, 5)	

5. These verbs take an object + infinitive (type 5); if they take any other constructions as well, they are shown in brackets:

ask (2)	command (1)	direct (1)	instruct (1)
invite (1)	order (1, 3)	persuade (3)	tell (1, 3)
warn (1, 3)			

See also
Unit 15 – Verb + object + infinitive
Unit 24 – Verbs of speaking: **say**, **tell**, **talk**, **speak** and **discuss**
Unit 37 – Reported speech

UNIT 26
Verbs of the senses

A. Sample sentences

- We are going to look at the sales figures later in the meeting, but first we're going to watch a short video about sales techniques.
- The figures for the last quarter look pretty good.
- A: How did their offer sound to you? It sounded unrealistic to me.
  B: I thought it sounded quite attractive.
- A: Jim, are you okay? You look absolutely white.
  B: I'm a bit shaky. I've just seen a bad accident at the plant.

B. Form

There are five senses: sight, hearing, smell, taste and touch. Each sense has three activities associated with it:

    intentional activity, e.g. **to look at** the figures
    unintentional activity, e.g. **to see** an accident
    describing the *current sensation*, e.g. **to look** attractive

Sense	Intentional activity	Unintentional activity	Current sensation
sight	**look at** (a static object) **watch** (a moving or changing object or activity)	**see**	**look**
hearing	**listen to**	**hear**	**sound**
smell	**smell**	**smell**	**smell**
taste	**taste**	**taste**	**taste**
feel	**touch/feel**	**touch/feel**	**feel**

C. Uses

1. Intentional activity:
   - Let's look at these figures in more detail. (the figures are a static object)
   - If we go over to the plant now we can watch the night shift take over from the day shift. ('taking over' is an activity involving change)
   - Sorry George, could you let John finish. I'd like to listen to what he has to say.
   - If you touch the surface before it has dried, it will leave a mark.
   - *Note:* I'm not interested in the detail. I'd just like to see the final figures. (experience visually, though without a lot of attention)

2. Unintentional activity:
   - I've just seen a bad accident at the plant.
   - I'm amazed! Did you hear what he said about our productivity?
   - I can smell something strange here. Is it gas?
3. Current sensation

   These verbs of sensation are followed by adjectives:
   - The figures for the last quarter look pretty good.
   - I think they may have to sell. Their results sounded terrible.
   - A: This is the new insulation material.
     B: To be honest, I expected something softer. It feels quite rough to me.

NOTES

1. We use **well** to describe health and **good** to describe positive attributes:
   He looks/feels very well. (healthy, not ill)
   cf. The plan looks very good in theory. (positive, not bad)
   The material feels very good. (not bad)
2. We do not use the present continuous for unintentional activity and current sensation verbs:
   Now do you see the column of figures on the right? That shows the overheads. (*not:* are you seeing)
   It's okay. You don't need to move the OHP. I can see quite well from here. (*not:* I am seeing)

See also
Unit 28 – Verbs + adjectives

UNIT 27
Arise, rise, raise, lie *and* lay

A. Sample sentences
- I'm sorry about this but an unforeseen problem has arisen at the plant. So, I'll have to go there immediately.
- The banks have raised the interest rates by another point. That means they have risen by four whole points this year.
- Now, this new fabric just lies on the floor – it doesn't need special fixing. After you've laid it, just make sure that no-one uses the room for twelve hours.

B. Form

V1	V2	V3
arise	arose	arisen
rise	rose	risen
raise	raised	raised
lie	lay	lain
lay	laid	laid

C. Uses

For more information on transitive and intransitive verbs, see Unit 21.

Arise
- A problem has arisen at the plant.

Arise is intransitive. It needs an active subject construction, not a dummy **it**:

   not: It has arisen a problem.

Rise
- Interest rates rose by 2 per cent last year.

Rise is intransitive:

   not: The banks rose interest rates last year

Raise
- The bank has agreed to raise our overdraft.

Raise is transitive:

   not: Our overdraft has raised by 10 per cent.

Lie

- This new material just lies on the surface.

Lie is intransitive:

not: First you lie the material on the surface.

Lay

- First lay the material on the floor.

Lay is transitive:

not: This new material just lays on the surface.

See also
Unit 21 – Active
Unit 68 – Describing trends

UNIT 28
Verbs + adjectives

A. Sample sentences

- The new product range is very interesting, particularly to our Far Eastern customers.
- Since he became marketing manager, John has become very good at encouraging the team to work together.
- With so much uncertainty over prices, the market has grown very nervous.
- I thought he already knew, but he sounded very surprised when I told him I was leaving.

B. Form

Verbs which take an adjective are *linking verbs*. We can divide them into:

1. *Current verbs*, which indicate what the subject is, e.g.:
   He **is/appears/seems/sounds** busy in his new job.
2. *Resulting verbs*, which indicate what the subject becomes, e.g.:
   The directors **became/got/grew** worried after the results were released.

Current verbs	Resulting verbs
be	become
remain	
appear	fall
feel	turn
look	
prove	
seem	
sound	
stay	
keep	get
smell	go
taste	grow
	run

C. Uses

1. Current verbs:
   - So far this year costs have remained/stayed stable.
   - Our new products have proved very popular in the USA.
   - The new engineer sounded very critical of our latest purchase.
   - If he asks you about the profits, just keep calm.

2. Resulting verbs:
   - The MD fell ill right after his summer holiday.
   - We hope he will get better before the next meeting.
   - I regret that the market has turned sour – just after our earlier success.
   - With the present volatility in the markets, share prices have run wild over the last few days.

See also
Unit 26 – Verbs of the senses

UNIT 29
Have, have got *and* get

A. Sample sentences

- They couldn't supply us on time because they didn't have the goods in stock.
- They have got a very good reputation for quality.
- We got the last delivery two weeks late. When can you get this delivery to us?

B. Form

	V1	V2	V3
Negative Question	**have** don't/doesn't have do/does S have	**had** didn't have did S have	**had** hasn't/haven't had have/has S had
Negative Question	**get** don't/doesn't get do/does S get	**got** didn't get did S get	**got/gotten** (Am.E.) hasn't/haven't got have/has S got

(S = subject)

Have is both a full verb and an auxiliary. (For the forms of the auxiliary see Unit 5 – The present perfect simple.)

The negative and question forms of the full verb **have** follow the normal patterns, as the table above shows.

Get is a full verb. The negative and question forms follow the normal patterns. So, the form **have got** is the present perfect of **get**.

C. Uses

1. The full verb **have**
   We use the appropriate forms of **do** and **did** in negatives and questions:
   - They don't have an agent in the Far East. (*not:* they haven't an agent in the Far East)
   - Do you have a factory in Italy? (*not:* Have you a factory in Italy?)
   - They didn't have the goods in stock. (*not:* they hadn't the goods in stock)
   - Did they have the goods in stock? (*not:* Had they the goods in stock?)

2. **Get**

In the present, past and past perfect, the main meaning of **get** is 'receive' or 'obtain':

- A: How often do you get a salary increase?
  B: I get an increase each year.
  A: And when did you get your last increase?
  B: I got it in July. By that time, the company had got a new pay policy.

Have got means 'have', i.e. with a *present* meaning:

- They have got a very good reputation for medium quality products.
- Have you got any new ideas for the next trade fair in Switzerland?
- *but:* Did you get any new ideas from the last trade fair in Switzerland. (*not:* Had you got any new ideas?)

See also

Unit 5 – The present perfect simple
Unit 6 – The present perfect continuous
Unit 7 – The past perfect

UNIT 30
Make *versus* do

A. *Sample sentences*

- The first half year's figures are very sound. We expect to make a good profit this year.
- We have been doing business with them for about four years now.
- A: We hope to make an agreement with them in the New Year.
  B: So soon? Have you done all your research into their activities?

B. *Form*

V1	V2	V3
make	made	made
do	did	done

C. *Uses*

There are no fixed rules about the meanings of **make** and **do**. Generally, we use **make** when there is an end-product, e.g. make a profit, make a mistake; and we use **do** when the activity is an end in itself, e.g. do business, do a job. Below is a list of common combinations.

1. **do**

the accounts/	repairs	business	damage
budget/forecast	a favour	good	a job
an exercise	a service	work	wrong

2. **make**

an apology	an appointment	arrangements	a budget/forecast
certain	a choice	a complaint	a decision
an effort	an enquiry	an excuse	friends (with)
a loss	a mistake	money	an offer
a profit	progress	a report	sure
a trip	(someone) welcome		work (for others)

NOTE

Notice the difference between these sentences:

> We do all the forecasts in November. (= **do** the activity)
> I am going to make a forecast at the next meeting. (= present the end-product)

See also
Unit 15 – Verb + object + infinitive

UNIT 31
Verb + preposition

A. Sample sentences

- Your presentation should consist of a short introduction, an overview, a main part, a summary and a conclusion.
- We have not decided on the exact format of the final product yet.
- Our price increase next year will partly depend on this year's inflation.
- A number of changes have been announced. Paul Bailey is going to take over the finance department.
- I'm afraid we can't rely on receiving the goods in time for October shipment.

B. Form

Prepositional verb phrases take two forms.

1. verb + preposition + prepositional object
   decide on   **the exact format**

2. verb + preposition + V1 . . . *ing*
   rely   on   **receiving**

NOTE

Where a preposition is followed by a verb, the verb form is always V1 . . . *ing*.

C. Uses

Below are some of the more common prepositional verbs.
agree with someone/something:
  - I agree with you entirely.
agree to something (= accept):
  - They have agreed to our proposal to speed up the whole project.
allow for something:
  - In the winter we must allow for delays of up to three weeks.
amount to something:
  - The consultancy fees amounted to more than we had expected.
apply for something:
  - We have just applied for membership of the European Marketing Scheme.
apologise for something:
  - I must apologise for keeping you all waiting.
approve of someone/something.
  - After watching the way George handled the crisis, I have to say I completely approve of his action.

attend to someone/something:
- I will attend to this matter as soon as possible.
  (*Note:* to attend a meeting)

complain (to someone) **about** someone/something:
- I'm going to complain to them about their poor delivery.

conform to something:
- All our products conform to European standards.

consent to something:
- They have consented to a display of their new products at the show.

consist of something:
- The equipment consists of three main parts.

depend on something:
- My answer depends on who is asking the question.

hear about something:
- Have you heard about the new appointment?

hear from someone:
- I hope to hear from you after you have looked at our proposal.

hope for something:
- We are hoping for a big improvement in productivity next year.

insist on something:
- They have insisted on putting back the date of signature.

look at someone/something:
- Have you had a chance to look at our proposal yet?

look for someone/something:
- We are looking for enthusiastic agents in all parts of Europe.

look forward to something:
- We are all looking forward to meeting you.

pay (someone) **for** something:
- We must pay them for the spare parts before the end of the month.

refer to something:
- If you refer to the appendix at the end of the contract, you will find all the numbers of the components.

rely on someone/something:
- You can rely on them; they are totally dependable.

succeed in something:
- Congratulations! You have succeeded in getting the Saudi contract.

think about something (= concentrate on):
- At present we are thinking about your offer and will get back to you shortly.

think of something (= consider):
- We are thinking of setting up a joint venture, but we would like some more information about the trading possibilities first.

wait for someone/something:
- We must contact them; they are waiting for our answer.

NOTE

We do not use a preposition after these verbs:

answer: Can I answer that question/you at the end of my presentation?
ask: Excuse me. I'd like to ask you a question, please.
        ('you' = indirect object; 'a question' = direct object)
call/phone/ring: I'll call/phone/ring you later.
                   I'll call/phone/ring the office later.
discuss: We can discuss this matter tomorrow.
enter: Don't enter this area without protective clothing.
meet: I met their general manager at the talk. (Br.E.)
        I met with their general manager at the talk. (Am.E.)
reach: We expect profits to reach £500,000 this year.
suit: Does 4 o'clock next Friday suit you?
tell: We will tell you later today if you have got the promotion.

See also
Unit 12 – Verb . . . *ing*
Unit 24 – Verbs of speaking: **say**, **tell**, **talk**, **speak** and **discuss**

UNIT 34
Sentence types – simple and complex

A. *Sample sentences*

- The company makes men's clothes.
- They have their HQ in Brussels but manufacture their products in Portugal.
- They use only two subcontractors because they prefer to keep strict control of the quality.

B. *Form*

A simple sentence comprises just one clause, i.e. with one verb phrase:

> The company **makes** men's clothes.

A complex sentence consists of more than one clause, i.e. with more than one verb phrase. We connect the clauses by *co-ordination*, *subordination* or a *relative pronoun*.

> They **have** their HQ in Brussels **but manufacture** their products in Portugal. (co-ordination with **but**)
>
> They **use** only two subcontractors **because** they **prefer** to keep strict control of the quality. (subordination with **because**)
>
> We**'ve moved** to Tokyo, **which is** certainly a very expensive place to live. (connection with **which**)

C. *Uses*

1. A simple sentence can be a statement, a question, a command or an exclamation:
   - The company makes men's clothes. (statement)
   - When can they start production? (question)
   - Don't start up the machine yet. (command)
   - What a mess they've made! (exclamation)
2. We can use co-ordination to connect clauses with the co-ordinating conjunctions **and, or, but**
   - We can make these components or buy them in from a local manufacturer.
3. We can use subordination to connect clauses with subordinating conjunctions, e.g. **when, though, because**:
   - They use only two subcontractors because they prefer to keep strict control of the quality.

NOTES

1. You can use a simple statement or question in a presentation to get the audience's attention:

The overheads have been too high.

Why do we need a new purchasing policy?

2. Co-ordination is more vague and less emphatic than subordination.

We made a loss last year and decided to review our make/buy policy and called in a consultant and he advised us to . . .

cf. As we made a loss last year, we decided to review our make/buy policy. So we called in a consultant who advised us to . . .

Subordination reduces the subordinated clause to a less important role.

3. Relative pronoun connectors (**who** and **which**) have an unemphatic connecting effect, sometimes similar to **and**:

They have given the job to Paul, who will be very efficient, I am sure.

They have given the job to Paul, and he will be very efficient, I am sure.

4. After a co-ordinating conjunction we can omit the following sentence elements, if they are the same as in the main clause:

the subject
the auxiliary or modal verb
the **to** from the infinitive

We can make these components or buy them in from a local manufacturer ('we can' is omitted).

We ought either to make these components or buy them in from a local manufacturer ('to' is omitted).

UNIT 35
Connecting ideas

A. *Sample sentences*

- The company was established ten years ago, at a time when manufacturing in this region was in decline. Therefore it was quite easy for us to recruit personnel. In addition, the government's incentive schemes made it attractive for us to open up here, especially since no tax was payable in the first three years.

B. *Form*

There are four main ways of connecting clauses together.
1. Co-ordination with **and**, **or**, **but** (see Unit 34).
2. Subordination with a subordinating conjunction, e.g. **when**, **though**, **because** (see Unit 36).
3. General purpose connectors with **who** and **which** (see Unit 39).
4. Adverbial connectors, e.g. **so**, **yet**, **then**. Here the clauses are separated either by a full-stop (.) or a semicolon (;), and then connected by an adverbial connector:

> . . . at a time when manufacturing in this region was in decline. *Therefore* it was quite easy for us to recruit personnel. *In addition*, the government's incentive schemes made it attractive for us to open up here.

C. *Uses*

We can use the three connecting methods to express the same sentences and ideas. The effect, however, is different.

> They only moved their headquarters here two years ago *but* moved out last year. (more vague and less emphatic)
> *Although* they only moved their headquarters here two years ago they moved out last year. (subordinated clause is reduced to a less important role)
> They only moved their headquarters here two years ago; *however*, they moved out last year. (typical in longer stretches of language to indicate the relationships between sentences and ideas)

Below are some of the more common adverbial connectors.

Cause:	therefore
	so
Contrast:	yet
	however
Condition:	then
	in that case
Comparison:	similarly
	in the same way

Concession:	anyway
	at any rate
Contradiction:	in fact
	actually
	as a matter of fact
Alternation:	instead
	alternatively
Addition:	also
	in addition
	too
Summary:	to sum up
	overall
	in brief/short
Conclusion:	in conclusion
	finally
	lastly
Equivalence:	in other words
	that means
	namely
Inclusion:	for example
	for instance
	such as
	as follows
Highlight:	in particular
	especially
Generalisation:	usually
	normally
	as a rule
	in general
Stating the obvious:	obviously
	naturally
	of course

See also
Unit 67 – Connecting and sequencing ideas

UNIT 36
Subordinate clauses

A. *Sample sentences*

- At the AGM the chairman said that he saw a tough year ahead. After he had made his short speech he invited questions from the floor so that the shareholders could get whatever other information they wanted. As the results had been good, no-one wanted to say much.

B. *Form*

A *subordinate clause* depends on a main clause – it cannnot stand by itself as a sentence.

```
┌──────── Subordinate clause ────────┐ ┌──────── Main clause ────────┐
```
After he had made his short speech he invited questions from the floor.

1. A subordinate clause starts with one of the following:
   a. **that**, e.g. The chairman said **that** he saw a tough year ahead.
   b. a subordinating conjunction, e.g. **As** the results had been good, no-one wanted to say much.
   c. a **wh-** word, e.g. I don't know **who** will take his place.
   d. an infinitive + **to**, e.g. we went there **to discuss** the contract
   e. a verb . . . *ing*, e.g. **having** bought the company, they restructured it
   f. a verb . . . *ed*, e.g. made by us, that product could have a future
   g. inversion, e.g. Should the agent default on the agreement, we will take legal action. (See Unit 10)
2. A subordinate clause contains:

   a finite verb in the active or passive:

   > The chairman said that he **saw** a tough year ahead.

   a non-finite verb, i.e. infinitive, verb . . . *ing* or verb . . . *ed*

   > We have come **to discuss** the new terms

Note the uses of the subjunctive:
1. The possible use of the subjunctive verb forms in **that** clauses after verbs such as:

   demand   require   insist   suggest   be necessary/obligatory

   > They suggested that he **come** for an interview the following week.
   > It is necessary that you all **be** on time for the meeting.

   The subjunctive has the form of V1 in all persons. We use the subjunctive mainly in formal style; in informal style we use **should** + infinitive:
   > They suggested that he **should come** for an interview the following week.
   > It is necessary that you **should** all **be** on time for the meeting.
2. The **were** subjunctive in clauses of condition and contrast:
   > If I **were** you, I would accept their offer immediately.

C. Uses

Below are the main types of subordinate clause.

1. Cause or reason (see Unit 41):
   - The company closed *because they couldn't become profitable*.
2. Condition (see Unit 10):
   - *If they hadn't overspent*, they could have survived.
3. Contrast (see Units 40 and 72):
   - *Although they made a profit in the first five years*, they then started to over-spend and went into the red.
4. Purpose:
   - They decreased their overheads *so that the company would be attractive to buyers*.
5. Result (see Units 41 and 77):
   - The finance manager had earned enough money *so (that) he could retire*.
   Note that this is different from the adverbial connector of reason **so**:
   - The finance manager had earned enough money: *so he could retire*.
6. Time (see Unit 43):
   - He left *when the receiver was called in*.
7. Reported speech (see Unit 37):
   - He said *that he would do everything in his power to solve the problem*.
8. Reported questions (see Unit 37):
   - The receiver wanted to know *why the debtor situation had become so bad*.
9. Relative clauses (see Unit 39):
   - First they repaid the banks *which had given short-term loans*.

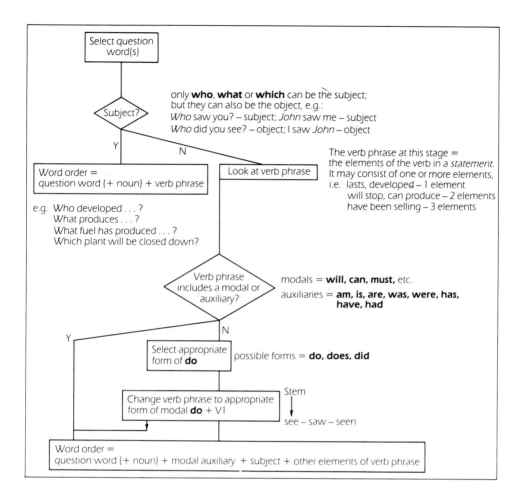

2. Indirect questions

Indirect questions comprise:

> a question word (**wh-**, **if** or **whether**)
> a question but with the verb in statement word order:

>> I'd like to know when you plan to deliver the equipment. (*not*: do you plan)
>> But could you tell me what else I could do? (*not*: could I do)

3. Statement questions

There are two types of statement question:

> a statement with rising intonation:
>> Jim, you bought this equipment?
> a statement + question tag:
>> Jim, you bought this equipment, didn't you?
>> Jim, you didn't buy this equipment, did you?

C. Uses

1. Direct questions
   Below are the main **wh-** questions according to question word.

   - Asking about people:
     - Who authorised the purchase? (**who** asks about the subject)
     - Who(m) did you meet at the trade fair? (in normal speech we use **who** to ask about the object; in formal speech and writing we use **whom**)
     - Who(m) did you buy this from? (in normal speech we use **who** to ask about the prepositional object; in formal speech and writing we use **whom**)
     - From whom did you buy this? (**whom** asks about the prepositional object. This structure is more formal than the previous one.)
   - Asking about things:
     - Which work station isn't functioning? (**which** + noun asks about the subject)
     - What have you decided? (**what** asks about the object)
   - Asking about the time:
     - When did they say the goods would be shipped?
     - (At) what time/When will the meeting start? (specific clock time)
   - Asking about the place:
     - Where are we going to hold the next sales conference?
   - Asking for the reason:
     - Why are you asking that question?
   - Asking about the length of time:
     - How long have you been working for ABC?
     - How long does it take you to get to work in the morning? (*not:* How long time?)
   Note: **How long** refers to time or dimension (see below)
   - Asking about distance:
     - How far do you live from your office?
   - Asking about frequency:
     - How often do you need to take on temporary staff?
   - Asking about manner:
     - How did you manage to persuade them to accept our offer?
   - Asking about quantity and amount:
     - How many people applied for the post? (asking about quantity (the subject))
     - How much did the advertisement cost? (asking about amount (the object))
   - Asking about dimensions and specifications:
     - How big/long/wide/deep/high will the tunnel be?
     - How fast can it run?

2. Indirect questions are used in:
   - Reported questions (see Unit 37):
     - He asked which equipment they had bought.
   - Polite requests (see Unit 82):
     - Could you tell me which equipment you bought?

3. Statement questions (+ question tag) are used to ask for confirmation.
   - Asking for confirmation of a positive statement:
     - Jim, you bought this equipment?
     - Jim, you bought this equipment, didn't you?

— Asking for confirmation of a negative statement:
  - Jim, you didn't buy this equipment?
  - Jim, you didn't buy this equipment, did you?

See also
Unit 37 – Reported speech
Unit 82 – Requesting information and action

UNIT 39
Relative clauses

A. *Sample sentences*
- The company which produces these parts has moved into this area.
- ABC, which produces these parts, has just closed its local office.
- Peter Jones, who heads the R&D department, will be able to answer that question.
- The person who can answer your question will be back later this afternoon.
- The company where this was designed has gone out of business.
- We intend to make further investments at a time when the economic conditions are more favourable.

B. *Form*

There are two types of *relative clause*:

> *defining* relative clauses
> *non-defining* relative clauses

We can distinguish them by the punctuation. Non-defining clauses are enclosed by commas; defining clauses are not.

| | Defining and non-defining | | Defining only |
	Personal	Non-personal	Personal and non-personal
subjective	who	which	that
objective	who(m)	which	that, Ø(no pronoun)
genitive	whose	of which/whose	
locative		where	
temporal		when	

> The company **which produces these parts** has moved into this area. (defining; no commas)
> Peter Jones, **who heads the R&D department**, will be able to answer that question. (non-defining; commas)

C. *Uses*

Relative clauses are subordinate clauses (see Unit 37) which provide information about a noun or noun phrase.

There are two types of relative clause: defining and non-defining. Defining relative clauses provide essential information which restricts or clarifies the meaning of the preceding noun or noun phrase by specifying its meaning more clearly.

- The person *who can answer your question* will be back later this afternoon.

'Who can answer your question? identifies the person; without this essential information, the sentence has a very different meaning.

Non-defining relative clauses provide additional, non-essential information.

- ABC, which produces these parts, has just closed its local office.

'which produces these parts' provides additional, non-essential information; without this information the basic meaning of the sentence remains the same.

1. Talking about people (personal):
   - The consultant who/that did this report has left the organisation. (subjective – defining)
   - John Peters, who supervised the study, is out of the country. (subjective – non-defining)
   - We don't need to interview those employees who(m)/that/Ø we have discussed already. (objective – defining)
   - We have talked to Andrea Green, who(m) we considered the best candidate. (objective – non-defining)
   - We think that Sarah Graham, with whom we discussed the matter yesterday, can best help us. (objective after preposition – non-defining)
   - And finally let me introduce a man whose face is known to most of us. (genitive – defining)
   - And this is Paul Davies, whose company supplies our valves. (genitive – non-defining)
2. Talking about things (non-personal):
   - We would like to see a machine which/that can produce the highest quality printing. (subjective – defining)
   - I'm afraid that the HP202, which can produce this quality, is out of stock at the moment. (subjective – non-defining)
   - We don't need to discuss those machines which/that/Ø you can't supply within two weeks. (objective – defining)
   - We think that the HP202, which you can supply within two weeks, suits our needs best. (objective – non-defining)
   - We are not interested in devices whose spare parts/the spare parts of which are not available in this country. (genitive – defining)
   - And finally we have the HP203, whose capacity/the capacity of which is much higher than the HP202. (genitive – non-defining)
3. Talking about places (locative):
   - I know a restaurant in the centre of Lisbon where they serve excellent lobster. (defining)
   - This site, where the old factory stood, has been completely redeveloped. (non-defining)
4. Talking about the time (temporal):
   - I'm afraid they haven't informed us of the exact time when the certificate will be issued. (defining)
   - We are currently recruiting managers in their third stage of development, when they reach about forty. (non-defining)

NOTES

1. The relative pronoun after **the reason**:

    I really don't know the reason *why/that* they moved up north.

    The reason *that/why* they have such a good reputation is because they consistently maintain quality.

    (*not:* the reason because)

2. The relative pronoun after **all**, **each**, **every** and compounds:

    We have contacted all the suppliers (*that*) we identified.

    We are very proud of everything (*that*) we have achieved.

    Each time (*that*) we meet, we discuss exactly the same points.

UNIT 40
Clauses of contrast

A. Sample sentences

- Advertising is a very powerful recruitment medium but it is also very expensive.
- Though local advertising is effective for supervisory posts, for middle and senior management we recommend national advertising.
- Some of the daily papers provide a specialist recruitment section, while/ whereas others don't.
- It is interesting that specialist journals are very effective ways to gain publicity even though they have a relatively small readership.

B. Form

Clauses of contrast are subordinate clauses (see Unit 37) which provide information which contrasts with the main clause.

Clauses of contrast start with either the *co-ordinating conjunction* **but** (see Unit 34) or a *subordinating conjunction* (see Unit 36). The main subordinating conjunctions are:

though   **although**   **even though**   **while**   **whereas**

Co-ordination is more vague and less emphatic than subordination:

Local advertising is cheap **but** national advertising is more effective.

Subordination reduces the subordinated clause to a less important role:

Although local advertising is cheap, it is not as effective as national advertising.

We can only use **while** and **whereas** to contrast equivalent ideas.

While local papers are cheap to advertise in, they don't have a wide readership.
(*not:* While the local papers are cheap to advertise in, we decided to use the national press.)

C. Uses

Clauses of contrast present a situation which is unexpected or surprising in view of the information in the main clause.

1. Contrast with **but**:
   - Advertising is a very powerful recruitment medium but it is also very expensive.
   - They have their HQ in Brussels but manufacture their products in Portugal. (omission of subject – see Unit 34)
2. Contrast with **though, although** and **even though**:
   - Though/although it is expensive, we have decided to advertise nationally.
   Even though is more emphatic than **though** or **although**:
   - Even though it is very expensive, we have decided to advertise internationally. (*not:* Even it is very expensive, we have decided to advertise internationally.)

3. Contrast with **while** and **whereas** to contrast equivalent ideas:
    - While local papers are cheap to advertise in, they don't have a wide readership.

NOTES

1. Subordinate clauses with **though, although** and **even though** can come before or after the main clause:

    > Though/although it is expensive, we have decided to advertise nationally.
    > We have decided to advertise nationally, though/although it is expensive.

2. Subordinate clauses with **while** and **whereas** can come before or after the main clause and, if totally parallel in construction, can be reversed.

    > Local papers have a small circulation, while national papers have a large circulation.
    > While national papers have a large circulation, local papers have a small circulation.
    > National papers have a large circulation, while local papers have a small circulation.
    > While local papers have a small circulation, national papers have a large circulation.

See also
Unit 72 – Comparing and contrasting ideas

UNIT 41
Clauses of cause or reason

A. Sample sentences
- As this document is confidential, please look after it carefully.
- Since we don't want anyone to know of our plans in advance, I will make my first statement tomorrow.
- I will consider the question of jobs first because this is your highest priority.

B. Form
Clauses of cause or reason are subordinate clauses (see Unit 37) which explain the information in the main clause.

Clauses of cause or reason start with a subordinating conjunction (see Unit 36). The main subordinating conjunctions are:

because   **as**   **since**

C. Uses
Clauses of cause or reason answer the question 'why?'; they present the reason for the information in the main clause.
- A: Why are we discussing this point first?
  - B: Because it is the highest priority.

Because, **as** and **since** have the same meaning and take the same construction.
- Because/As/Since the economic climate has improved, we intend to invest in new plant and machinery.

NOTE

After **because** we need a finite verb; after **because of** we need a noun phrase:
- Because the situation has now changed, we can discuss the matter.
  - *cf.*   Because of the changed situation, we can discuss the matter. (*not:* Because the changed situation, we can discuss the matter.)

See also
Unit 77 – Cause and effect

UNIT 42
Clauses of purpose

A. Sample sentences

- We have changed the management team (in order) to make the company more efficient.
- We have redesigned our product literature so as to change our image.
- We have modified the product so that it meets customer requirements.
- We have decided to introduce inhouse training in order that we might develop our own programmes.

B. Form

Clauses of purpose are subordinate clauses (see Unit 37).
Clauses of purpose comprise

a subordinating conjunction followed by a finite verb (see Unit 36):

We have modified the product **so that** it **meets** customer requirements.

infinitive + **to** (see Unit 36):

We have changed the management team **(in order) to make** the company more efficient.

for + noun followed by an infinitive + **to**:

For the project to be completed by the end of May we need to start now.
(= so that the project can be completed by the end of May we need to start now)

The main subordinating conjunctions are:

so that   **that**   **in order that**

Before the infinitive + **to** you can put:

in order (to)   **so as (to)**

Note the negative forms:
So as not to waste time, we have circulated the papers before the meeting.
We are closing the plant early this Christimas **in order not to run** it unprofitably.

C. Uses

Clauses of purpose answer the question 'why?' or 'what for?'. They present the purpose of the information in the main clause:
- A: What are we discussing this now for?
  B: So that we can finally close this subject.
- A: Why are you closing the plant early this Christmas?
  B: In order not to run it unprofitably.

---

1. We use **to, in order to** and **so as to** + infinitive to talk about the doer's purpose
    - We have opened an office in Paris to develop the French market. (our purpose is to develop)
2. We use **that, so that** or **in order that** where the subject of the clauses is different.
    - They opened an office in Paris so that we could concentrate on the home market.
3. We use **to** + infinitive to talk about the purpose of something
    - The meeting is to enable both sides to present their problems.
    When we are talking about the purpose of equipment we can say
    - This button here is to reset the machine.
    - This button here is for resetting the machine. (for + verb . . . *ing*)

NOTE

The following sentences are *wrong*:

> We opened an office in Paris *for* develop the French market. (to develop)
> We opened an office in Paris *for to* develop the French market. ((in order) to develop)
> We opened an office in Paris *for* develop*ing* the French market (to develop)

See also
Unit 13 – Infinitive

UNIT 43
Clauses of time

A. Sample sentences

- Before you can start trading you need to register your company.
- After you have registered your company you will receive a certificate.
- Having signed all the necessary documents, we left to visit our first client.
- While a person is employed, you must supply his or her details to this office.
- Once formed, a company must keep official records of its income.
- After setting up a joint venture, it is essential to maintain regular contact with the new office.

B. Form

Clauses of time are subordinate clauses (see Unit 37). Clauses of time comprise

a subordinating conjunction followed by a finite verb (see Unit 36):

Before you **can start** trading you need to register your company.

a subordinating conjunction followed by a non-finite verb (see Unit 36):

After returning from my sales trip, I wrote a report on the visit.

a non-finite verb – verb . . . *ing* or verb . . . *ed* (see Unit 36):

Having signed all the necessary documents, we left to visit our first client.

We use the following subordinating conjunctions with finite verbs:

after	as	before	once	since	till
until	when(ever)	while/whilst	now (that)	as long as	as soon as

After you **have registered** your company you will receive a certificate.

We use the following subordinating conjunctions with verb . . . *ing*:

after	before	since	until	when(ever)	while

Before going on my sales trip, I phoned all the clients I intended to visit.

We use the following subordinating conjunctions with verb . . . *ed*:

once	until	when(ever)	while

Once formed, a company must keep official records of its income.

C. Uses

Clauses of time ask 'when?'; they present the time of the information in the main clause.
- A: When do you need to register your company?
  B: Before you start trading.

We use clauses of time to show that the time clause happens:

- earlier than the main clause
- at the same time as the main clause
- later than the main clause
- at a non-specific time

1. Earlier than the main clause:
   - Before giving/you give a presentation, make sure you have prepared it thoroughly.
2. At the same time as the main clause:
   - When giving/you give your presentation, look at your audience.
   - While/As he was demonstrating the equipment, he noticed a major design fault.
   - I have worked for ABC since I moved to the area. (start of work for ABC was at the same time as moving to the area)
   - We can give you this document as long as this special offer stands.
3. Later than the main clause:
   - After/Once/As soon as you have finished your presentation, invite your audience to ask questions.
   - I stayed in Switzerland until/till the contract was signed.
   - (After) having selected a number of suppliers, invite them to make their offers.
4. At a non-specific time:
   - Please contact me whenever you are in the area.

NOTE

We use the present or present perfect with *before, after, once, until* and *when(ever)* for future reference:

> We will finalise our offer before you visit us next week (*not:* before you will visit us)

> We will contact you after we receive/have received your offer. (*not:* after we will receive)

See also
Unit 62 – Numerals
Unit 63 – Time

UNIT 44
-ing and -ed clauses

A. *Sample sentences*

- Having left ABC, I went to work for P&M.
- Referring back to what I said, it is clear that our weak point is quality.
- Manufactured in Italy, this product displays the finest design features.
- While stored in the warehouse, the goods are constantly monitored.

B. *Form*

-ing and **-ed** clauses are non-finite subordinate clauses (see Unit 36).
1. We can put a subordinating conjunction before the clause (see Unit 36):
    (*While*) *stored* in the warehouse, the goods are constantly monitored.
2. We assume that the subject of the subordinate clause is the same as the subject of the main clause:
    Launched two years ago, the company has gained a large market share.
    Note: This rule is often broken:
    Since joining the company, my prospects have certainly improved.

C. *Uses*

-ing and **-ed** clauses (without a subordinating conjunction) can be interpreted in different ways:
- Reduced by 10 per cent, this is a bargain.
This can mean *if* reduced, *when* reduced or *because* reduced. So, we often include the subordinating conjunction to make the meaning clear.
1. Condition (see Unit 10):
    - If regularly serviced, this machine should provide years of service.
2. Contrast (see Unit 40):
    - Although having broken into the Far East market, the company is still in financial difficulties.
3. Cause or reason (see Unit 41):
    - Having missed the plane, I had to wait till the following day for a connection.
4. Time (see Unit 43):
    - Until signed by both parties, this agreement is not a legally binding document.
5. Manner:
    - By reducing prices dramatically, Brent regained market share.

See also
Unit 12 – Verb . . . *ing*

UNIT 45
Nouns

A. Sample sentences

- ABC have their headquarters in The Hague.
- The equipment is very simple to install.
- The machines will be in operation next week.
- Your board are expected to make a decision at the next meeting.

B. Form

We can classify nouns as shown in following chart.

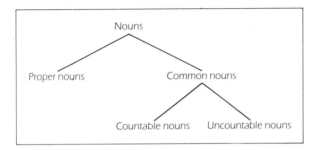

1. *Proper nouns* are names and are written with a capital letter, e.g. Great Britain, General Electric, Paul Smith. In exceptional cases they take *the*, e.g. The Hague, the USA, and the Bank of England (see below).
2. *Common nouns* can be divided into *countable* and *uncountable*. This distinction is a grammatical distinction, not a real-world distinction, e.g. money is grammatically uncountable (see below), but is clearly countable in reality!
   a. Countable nouns have a singular and a plural, e.g. machine/machines, or a plural only, e.g. people.
   b. Uncountable nouns have only one form. This may be grammatically singular, e.g. equipment, information, money, news and advice, or grammatically plural, e.g. personnel and police.
   A grammatically singular noun takes a singular verb; a grammatically plural noun takes a plural verb.
   > The information is in the brochure.
   > The personnel are very happy with the new premises.
   You cannot put **a/an** or a number in front of an uncountable noun. You cannot say an equipment, an information, a news; you can say a piece of equipment, an item of information/news.

NOTE

Singular countable nouns normally take a singular verb:

> The machine is operating.

Sometimes, however, a singular countable noun can take a plural verb when the noun is a collective noun, i.e. refers to 'more than one person', e.g.:

> The board are discussing that question now. (board = more than one person)

C. Uses

1. Proper nouns refer to unique people or objects, i.e. 'America' refers to one country and 'Paul Smith' (in a given conversation) refers to one person. The following proper nouns take the definite article.

   – Plural names:
   the Netherlands   the Midlands   the Alps   the Thomsons (the Thomson family)

   – Public institutions and facilities:
   the Hilton   the Odeon (cinema)   the British Museum

   – Newspapers:
   The Times   the *Daily Express*

2. Countable common nouns. Most common nouns are countable. They can take an indefinite or definite article, or no article at all (see Unit 55):
   - We have negotiated a bank loan.
   - We have renegotiated the bank loan.
   - At the moment it is difficult to get bank loans.

   The following nouns have only a plural form (**-s**) and take a plural verb:

archives	*contents*	*headquarters*	*savings*
arrears	*customs* (taxes)	*outskirts*	*surroundings*
assets (belonging to a company)	*funds* (money)	*premises* (buildings)	*thanks*

3. Uncountable common nouns

   – These nouns ending in -**ics** are usually singular:
   economics   *tactics*   *politics*   *mathematics*   *ethics*
   – *News* is always singular.
   – Substances are often singular, e.g. oil, butter, petrol, coal and wine. They can be used as countable nouns when they mean 'a type of':
   - We now sell three butters. (three types of butter)
   – The following nouns are uncountable singular:

accommodation	*advice*	*baggage*	*equipment*	*furniture*
information	*luggage*	*machinery*	*permission*	*progress*
traffic	*travel*	*trouble*	*weather*	*work*

   - We're planning to invest in new *machinery*. (uncountable)
   - We're planning to invest in new *machines*. (countable plural)

See also
Unit 55 – Articles
Unit 62 – Numerals

UNIT 46
Noun compounds

A. Sample sentences

- The profit bonus is one type of incentive that can be offered to employees.
- The sales forecast shows that we expect a 25 per cent increase in turnover for next year.
- We have managed to reduce the workforce by 12 per cent.
- Work-sharing is a system where two part-timers share one job.

B. Form

A noun compound comprises two or more nouns which are combined together into a phrase. A noun compound comprises:

> one or more modifying nouns + a head noun

The *modifying noun* acts like an adjective and gives more information about the head noun:

> A: We intend to pay a *bonus*. (head noun)
> B: What type of bonus?
> A: A *profit* bonus. (modifying noun)

1. The modifying noun, like an adjective, comes before the head noun
    > management development (= the development of management)
    > portfolio management (= the management of portfolios)
2. The modifying noun, like an adjective, is in the singular
    > car factory (= a factory which produces cars)
    > taxpayer (= a person who pays taxes)
    Note: Sales manager (= the manager responsible for sales; *not:* the manager responsible for sale)
3. There are no fixed rules about writing compounds
    > profit bonus (two separate words)
    > work-sharing (hyphenated)
    > taxpayer (one word)

As language changes, there is a tendency for new compounds to be formed and for familiar compounds to be written as one word. The following are all possible:

> work force   work-force   workforce

C. Uses

1. Noun compounds are shorter and more convenient than noun phrases:
    - a taxpayer versus a payer of taxes
2. Noun compounds are more concise – and therefore have greater impact – than noun phrases:
    - management development programmes versus programmes of development for management

3. Noun compounds can be ambiguous:
    *   criminal lawyer (a specialist in criminal law or a lawyer who is a criminal)
4. Noun compounds can become too long and difficult to understand:
    *   quality control management development officer (= officer for the development of management in the control of quality)

    It is more comprehensible to say:
    *   the management development officer responsible for quality control

See also
Unit 45 – Nouns

UNIT 47
Genitive forms

A. Sample sentences

- Many people feel that Britain's role has diminished as a world economic power.
- The organisation's trading position has improved this quarter.
- The opening of the new plant will create many employment opportunities.
- This quarter's results are better than expected.
- Paul's announcement came as a complete surprise to all of us.

B. Form

The genitive is written with an apostrophe (+ **s** if the noun is singular) or with the preposition **of**.

> this year**'s** results (= the results of this year)
> the last two quarters**'** results (= the results of the last two quarters)
> the development **of** a new distribution network
> the prices **of** all new products

C. Uses

1. We typically use the genitive with **'s** or **s'** with the following nouns

   - human nouns:
     - Paul's announcement
   - animal nouns:
     - the lion's share
   - time nouns:
     - the last two quarters' results
   - location nouns:
     - Britain's role   the country's development
   - organisation nouns, where an organisation is a group of people:
     - the audience's reaction   the board's decision
2. We use the genitive with **of** with things:
     - the end of the assembly line (*not:* the assembly line's end)
     - the development of management science
3. We can use either the apostrophe form or the **of** form with organisation nouns:
     - the company's results or the results of the company
     - the meeting's decision or the decision of the meeting

NOTES
1. The possessive pronoun **its** is not written with an apostrophe:
> The company has increased its profits substantially.
>> *cf.* It's surprising to see the substantial increase in profits.
2. When a proper noun ends in **s** we usually just add an apostrophe (but no **s**) to indicate possession:
> We regret to announce Mr Jones' resignation.

See also
Unit 45 – Nouns
Unit 56 – Pronouns

UNIT 48
Adjectives versus adverbs

A. Sample sentences
- This contract means that the year is off to a good start.
- This contract means that the year has started well.
- His resignation will have a serious effect on our reputation.
- His resignation will seriously affect our reputation.

B. Form
1. Many adjectives are derived from nouns or verbs:

Ending	Noun or verb	Adjective	Ending	Noun or verb	Adjective
-ite	define	definite	-(i)al	manager	managerial
				accident	accidental
-ful	use	useful	-less	hope	hopeless
-al	economy	economical	-ic	economy	economic
-ive	product	productive	-ous	number	numerous
-able/ible	agree	agreeable	-ing	interest	interesting
			-ed	interest	interested

2. Other adjectives, especially one- or two-syllable adjectives, do not have a suffix:

   good   bad   young   old   big   small

3. Most adverbs are derived from adjectives by adding **-ly** (adjectives ending in **-ic** add **-ally**):

   definite – definite**ly**   useful – useful**ly**   productive – productive**ly**
   dramatic – dramatic**ally**   systematic – systematic**ally**

   But: public – publicly

NOTES
1. Some adjectives end in **-ly**:
      lively   lovely   friendly   lonely

2. Some adjectives have the same form as adverbs:
      early   late   straight   hard   direct
      short   long   high   fast   wrong

      I intend to take the early flight to Paris. Then I can arrive early at your office.

3. Some adverbs ending in **-ly** have a different meaning from the adjective without **-ly**:

> He is a hard worker.
> He works hard.
> He hardly works. (= almost not at all)

4. Irregular forms:

> good – well

C. Uses

We use adjectives in the following instances.

1. To give more information about nouns:
   - The *recent* figures show a *sharp* increase in productivity.
     Which figures? – The recent figures
     What type of increase? – A sharp increase

   The adjective normally comes before the noun.

2. After the verb **be** (see Unit 23):
   - We are *pleased* about the takeover. (adjective + preposition)
   - We are *pleased* that the company was taken over. (adjective + **that**-clause)
   - We were *pleased* to hear about the takeover. (adjective + infinitive with **to**)

3. After verbs of the senses (see Unit 26):
   - He sounds very *pleasant* on the phone.

4. After linking verbs (see Unit 28):
   - Profits have remained *stable* for the last two quarters.

We use adverbs in the following instances:

1. To give more information about a verb:
   - Profits dropped *dramatically* last year.
   - How did they drop? – Dramatically

2. To give more information about an adjective:
   - The figures show an *extremely* sharp increase in productivity.
   - How sharp? – Extremely sharp

3. To give more information about an adverb:
   - They installed the equipment *fairly* quickly.
   - How quickly? – Fairly quickly

4. To give more information about a sentence:
   - *Finally*, let's look at the forecast for next year.

NOTE

Be careful of the difference in meaning between these adjectives and adverbs:

economic (in the economy)	*economical* (money-saving)
interesting (to someone)	*interested* (in something)
late (not early)	*lately* (recently)
present (current)	*presently* (soon)

See also
Unit 23 – **Be**
Unit 26 – Verbs of the senses
Unit 28 – Verbs + adjectives

UNIT 49
Adjective modification with adverbs

A. *Sample sentences*

- We have had an extremely good year as far as profits are concerned.
- He has done an absolutely marvellous job on the new product range.
- It is highly unlikely that we will open the new office before January.
- R&D have reported that a self-monitoring device is technically possible.

B. *Form*

Most adverbs are derived from adjectives by adding **-ly**; adjectives ending in **-ic** add **-ally**:

definite – definite**ly**	useful – useful**ly**	productive – productive**ly**
dramatic – dramatic**ally**	systematic – systematic**ally**	

C. *Uses*

Adverbs modify adjectives in two ways:

- by intensifying their meaning, e.g. an *extremely* good year, *reasonably* good results
- by indicating a point of view, e.g. *technically* possible (= possible from a technical point of view)

1. Intensifying adverbs:
    - We have had a *fairly* good year.
      How good? – Fairly good.

We can classify intensifying adverbs on a scale from 'totally' to 'moderately', where 'totally' intensifies the adjective to a high degree and 'moderately' intensifies the adjective slightly.

wholly
totally
completely
fully
absolutely
entirely

extremely
highly

very

fairly
reasonably
quite
moderately

2. Point of view adverbs:

  It was *commercially* necessary to develop a new product.

  Necessary from which point of view? From a commercial point of view.

NOTES

1. *Real* versus *really*:

  He was real interested in the job. (Am.E. – informal)

  He was really interested in the job. (Br.E. and Am.E.)

2. The position of *quite*:

  Quite an important person

  Quite a big company

See also

Unit 48 – Adjectives versus adverbs

Unit 68 – Describing trends

Unit 70 – Asserting and toning down information

UNIT 50
Comparison of adjectives

A. Sample sentences
- Brotherton have been in the market longer than Benton.
- Mansell have the biggest market share.
- Benton say that they can offer the earliest deliveries.
- Mansell's products are the most expensive, but also the most reliable.

B. Form

1. Adjectives with one syllable:

long	longer	the longest
big	bigger	the biggest
low	lower	the lowest
late	later	the latest

2. Two-syllable adjectives ending in **y**, **ow**, and **le**:

easy	easier	the easiest
narrow	narrower	the narrowest
simple	simpler	the simplest

3. Other two-syllable adjectives and longer adjectives:

reliable	**more** reliable	the **most** reliable
expensive	**more** expensive	the **most** expensive
profitable	**more** profitable	the **most** profitable

4. Irregular adjectives:

good	better	best	little	less	least
bad	worse	worst	far	farther	farthest
much	more	most		further	furthest

C. Uses

1. Comparison of objects

   - to compare two objects:
     - Brotherton are *more* reliable than Benton.
     - Brotherton are *the more* reliable. (of two)
   - to compare more than two objects:
     - Mansell are *the most* reliable. (of the three companies)
   - to compare an object and a definite standard:
     - We are productive, but to compete we must become *more* productive.

2. Modification of comparison. We can use an adverb before a comparative adjective to indicate the degree of comparison
   - Brotherton have a *much* bigger market share than Benton.

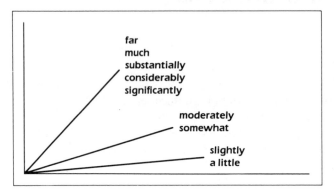

far
much
substantially
considerably
significantly

moderately
somewhat

slightly
a little

These words come before a comparative adjective.
   - Our profits were *considerably* better than expected.

NOTE

You cannot say:

Brotherton are more bigger than Mansell. (bigger)
Brotherton are much big than Mansell. (much bigger)

See also
Unit 48 – Adjectives versus adverbs
Unit 49 – Adjective modification with adverbs

UNIT 51
Expressions of frequency

A. Sample sentences

- We always hold our annual European group meetings in Frankfurt.
- Usually participants attend from all our European offices.
- I report to the product manager about product developments about once a month.
- When I worked in the States, I rarely travelled to Canada.

B. Form

We can divide expressions of frequency into:

indefinite frequency
definite frequency

1. We can classify expressions of indefinite frequency on a scale from 'always' to 'never', where 'always' = 100 per cent and 'never' = 0 per cent. These numbers are only a general indication, not exact values:

100%	always
95%	nearly always/almost always
90%	usually/normally/generally/regularly
75%	often/frequently
50%	sometimes
40%	occasionally
25%	rarely/seldom
10%	hardly ever/scarcely ever
0%	never

2. If we want to be more precise, we can use one of the following types of expression:

    once/twice/three times a day/week/month/year
    every hour/day/week/month/year
    hourly/daily/weekly/monthly/quarterly/annually or yearly

NOTE

Hourly/daily/weekly/monthly/quarterly/yearly are both adjectives and adverbs; *annually* is an adverb only (adjective = *annual*)

> I **meet** my deputy **daily** to discuss important matters. (adverb)
> I have a **daily meeting** with my deputy to discuss important matters. (adjective)

C. Uses

1. Questions about frequency:
   - How often do you hold business meetings?
2. Statements about frequency:
   - Indefinite frequency:
     - We always hold our annual European group meetings in Frankfurt. (normal position for adverbs of frequency is before the verb)
     - Sometimes we send out the invitations to the AGM at the beginning of August. (for emphasis *usually/normally/generally/regularly/often/frequently/sometimes/occasionally* can be put at the beginning of the sentence)
     - I am normally at work by 8 o'clock. (adverb of frequency after the verb **be**)
   - Definite frequency:
     - I report to the product manager about product developments about once a month. (normal position for expressions of frequency is at the end of the sentence)
     - Once a year I visit our distributors in Greece. (for emphasis the expression of frequency can be put at the beginning of the sentence)

NOTES

1. **Per** is official and formal:
   According to the contract we should receive one statement per month.
2. **Every** is always singular:
   We produce a new brochure every year. (*not*: every years)

See also
Unit 2 – The present simple
Unit 48 – Adjectives versus adverbs
Unit 61 – **Each, every** and compounds

UNIT 52
Degree with very, too *and* enough

A. *Sample sentences*

- Raw material costs have risen very rapidly over the last twelve months.
- We have appointed a very aggressive agency to develop a new marketing strategy.
- I'm afraid that there were too many mistakes on the last order; therefore we don't intend to use your company again.
- We won't have enough time to visit all the stands at the exhibition.
- We need a larger office; the present one isn't big enough.

B. *Form*

Very, **too** and **enough** are adverbs (see Unit 48).
Very and **too** come before the adjective or adverb:

> Raw material costs have risen **very rapidly**.
> It is **too soon** for us to make a decision.

The adverb **enough** comes after the adjective or adverb:

> Our present plant isn't **big enough**.

The determiner **enough** comes before the noun:

> We have **enough stocks** to last till the end of the month.

C. *Uses*

1. **Very** is a degree adverb; it intensifies the meaning of an adjective or adverb:
   - We have appointed a very aggressive agency.
   - Raw material costs have risen very rapidly.
2. The adverbs **too** and **enough** have related meanings. **Too** means 'more than enough' or 'more than acceptable':
   - The present office is too small. (it is not acceptable)
   Enough means that something is acceptable:
   - The present office is big enough. (it is acceptable)
   Compare **too** and **enough** in the following sentences:
   - The present office is too small.
   - The present office is not big enough.
   Too small means 'too small for us to work in'; **not big enough** means 'not big enough for us to work in'; therefore **too** and **enough** are by reference to a level, a person and an activity:

	level	person	activity
• This office is too	*small*	for *us*	to *work in*

   Often we do not mention the person and the activity because they are obvious from the context:
   - Your products are too expensive. (for me to buy)

3. The determiner **enough** also refers to a level:
- There are enough raw materials.

As with the adverb **enough**, often we do not mention the person and the activity:
- There are enough raw materials. (for us to continue production)

NOTE

Compare the meanings of **too** (more than enough), **enough** and **very** (extremely) in the following sentences:

His qualifications were very good, but not good enough for us.

Your qualifications were very good – in fact too good for us.

See also
Unit 49 – Adjective modification with adverbs

UNIT 53
So *versus* such

A. *Sample sentences*
- The quality was so low that we couldn't accept the delivery.
- Why has there been such a long delay in despatching the goods?

B. *Form*
We use **so** before an adjective or an adverb:

       The quality was **so low**.

       They finished the contract **so quickly**.

We use **such** before (an adjective +) a noun:

       Why has there been **such a (long) delay**?

Note the position of **such**:

       such a (reliable) supplier (before the indefinite article with countable singular nouns)

       such (reliable) suppliers (with countable plural nouns)

       such (reliable) information (with uncountable nouns)

C. *Uses*
1. As adverbs of degree (see Unit 52):
   - The quality was so low that we couldn't accept the goods. (= the quality was *too low* for us to accept the goods or the quality was *not high enough* for us to accept the goods)
2. To indicate the result:
   - They worked such long hours that they finished the project ahead of time. (with the result that they finished)
3. In emphatic statements or exclamations:
   - The factory was so clean!
   - The plant was such a mess!
4. In negative comparisons:
   - Their prices are not so high as I thought. (or not as high as)
5. Phrases with **so**:
   - *So long as* they continue to maintain their present price levels, we will deal with them. (time)
   - The report was accurate, *(in) so far as* it went. (extent)
   - We have completed three projects *so far*. (up to now)

See also

Unit 36 – Subordinate clauses

Unit 42 – Clauses of purpose

Unit 67 – Connecting and sequencing ideas

UNIT 54
Already, yet, again *and* still

A. Sample sentences
- I'm sorry to inform you that we have already appointed someone.
- Have you finished the project in Saudi yet?
- I hear you are selling your products in the Far East again.
- He is still running the company after all these years.

B. Form

Already, **yet**, **again** and **still** are adverbs of time.

1. We can put **already** at the end of the sentence:
   > We have appointed someone already.

   Note the other possible positions

   with the main verb **be**:
   > It is already clear that we have made a mistake (after **be**)

   with a modal or auxiliary:
   > The report has already been sent. (after the first modal or auxiliary)

   with other verbs:
   > We already receive that journal every month. (before the main verb)

2. **Yet** usually comes at the end of the sentence:
   > A: Have you finished the Saudi project yet?
   > B: Yes, but our people haven't returned yet.

3. **Again** usually comes at the end of the sentence:
   > We're recruiting a factory manager again.

4. **Still**

   with the main verb **be**:
   > The building is still under construction. (after **be**)

   with a modal or auxiliary:
   > Our new plant is still being built. (after the first modal or auxiliary)

   with other verbs:
   > We still visit the Milan Trade Fair every year. (before the main verb)

NOTES

1. When using personal pronouns you usually mention yourself last:

   My boss and I will be attending the conference. (*not:* I and my boss)
   One should ask oneself this question before applying for a job, not after. (one = indefinite pronoun, i.e. a person)

2. Reflexive pronouns:

   I did it myself. (I did it; not anybody else)
   I did it by myself. (without anyone else's help)

3. You can use **own** with personal pronouns to add emphasis:

   Our own products are of a much higher quality, as you will see.

UNIT 57
Demonstratives

A. Sample sentences

- I'd like to introduce my colleague. This is Trish Stott.
- Now I'd like to look at the figures. These are divided into the following categories.
- So those were the main points and that concludes my presentation.

B. Form

Demonstratives are words which point to something in the context – something near or something distant. They can be *pronouns* (see Unit 56) and *determiners*.

The forms of the demonstratives are as follows:

	Singular	Plural
Near reference	**this**	**these**
Distant reference	**that**	**those**

C. Uses

1. The demonstratives **this** and **that** can point *backwards* to something we mentioned earlier:
   - We launched the AB400 and this/that was a great success. (pronoun)
   - We launched the AB400 in January. This/that product has been targeted at the top end of the market. (determiner)
2. The demonstrative **this** can point *forwards* to something we are going to mention later.
   - This is the way that they are going to ensure we protect our business interests. (pronoun) First we will reduce all unnecessary costs. By unnecessary costs I mean these types of items: inventory, labour and other non-fixed overheads. (determiner)
3. The demonstratives **this** and **that** can point to something in the real world, i.e. outside the language:
   - I can offer two models in our present range that suit your needs. This one (here) can handle 200 items per minute; and that one (there) can handle 250.

NOTES

1. We use **that** and **those** before a relative clause:
   I'd like to ask those who are against the proposition to raise their hands now.
2. In colloquial speech we use the forward-pointing **this** to introduce a subject that we are going to describe more fully afterwards:
   So, we went into this bar in Barcelona, and you wouldn't believe what we saw.

UNIT 58
Some, any *and related words*

A. Sample sentences

- We intend to invest some of this year's profits in new plant, somewhere in the north-east.
- They don't want any advice on marketing; but they would like something on business plans in general.
- If anyone has any questions I will be happy to answer them now.
- I am not interested in any of their special offers.

B. Form

SOME WORDS Positive statements	**ANY** WORDS	
	Negative statements	Questions
Determiner I have **some** information	I do**n't** have **any** information	Do you have **any** information?
Pronoun I told **someone** in head office	I did**n't** tell **anyone** in head office	Did you tell **anyone**?
I'd like to ask **something**	I do**n't** want to ask **anything**	Would you like to ask **anything**?
Place adverb I've seen him **somewhere**	I have**n't** seen him **anywhere**	Have you seen him **anywhere?**
Time-when adverb I'll see him again **some time**	I wo**n't** **ever** see him again	Will I **ever** see him again?
Time-frequency adv. I **sometimes** go to the USA	I do**n't** **ever** go to the USA	Do you **ever** go to the USA?
Degree adverb I was **somewhat** surprised	I was**n't** **at all** surprised	Were you **at all** surprised?

NOTES

1. We can use **somebody** or **someone** as personal pronouns; similarly **anybody** can be used instead of **anyone**.
2. The negative with **ever** is the same as **never**:
   > I do*n't ever* go to the USA.
   > I *never* go to the USA.
3. With **some** we can't use **the**:
   > Some people (*not:* some the people)

C. Uses

1. Uses of **some** and compounds
   Some is a determiner and a pronoun; **someone** and **something** are pronouns; and other **some** compounds are adverbs. We use **some** words in:

   – positive statements:
     - There are some figures in this year's report. (determiner + plural countable noun)
     - We have received some information about the proposed takeover. (determiner + uncountable noun)
     - We intend to invest some of this year's profits in new plant. (pronoun)
     - There's someone on the phone for you. (pronoun)
     - The bank interest must be somewhere on the profit and loss account. (adverb)
   – polite offers in the question form:
     - Would you like to ask some other questions?

2. Uses of **any** and compounds
   The uses of **any** + compounds are parallel to the uses of **some** + compounds above: We use **any** words:

   – in negative statements:
     - I haven't seen any advertisements for the new job. (determiner + plural countable noun)
   – in direct questions (see Unit 38):
     - Does anyone have any questions? (pronoun; determiner + plural countable noun)
   – in **yes/no** indirect questions (see Unit 37):
     - I'd like to know whether anyone has any further details about the current expenses.
   – in conditional clauses (see Unit 10):
     - If by any chance anyone calls while I am away, please tell them to contact me in Sweden.
   – in comparisons after **-er**, **more** (see Unit 50), **less**, **as**, **too** (see Unit 52):
     - The results are better than anyone could have imagined.
     - The removal of the board has come too late for us to do anything about the present situation.

– to mean 'every' or 'all' (see Unit 61). **Any** + singular countable noun, e.g. any manager, or **any** + uncountable noun, e.g. any information.
- Any sales manager can sell this product (every sales manager or all sales managers)
- Any information would be much appreciated. (all information)

NOTE

We do not use **any** (unstressed) with singular countable nouns
        Does anyone have any questions (*not:* any question)

UNIT 59
Quantifiers with all, many, much, several, (a) few, (a) little *and* no

A. *Sample sentences*

- We have now inspected all the equipment in the plant.
- Unfortunately, many of your protection devices are not operating correctly.
- There is not much room for each operative, and we would recommend that you look into this as soon as possible.
- To be honest, we receive few complaints about our working conditions.
- There are no plans to close the plant.

B. *Form*

	Countable		Uncountable
	Singular	Plural	
↑	all the	all/all (of) the	all/all (of) the
		most (of the)	most (of the)
		many (of the)	much (of the)
	a lot of (the)	a lot of (the)	a lot of (the
		several (of the)	several (of the)
		a few (of the)	a little (of the)
		few (of the)	little (of the)
	no	no	no

NOTES
1. **A lot of** and **lots of** are more colloquial than **many** and **much**.
2. The use of the definite article:

> **All** equipment needs replacing. (understood from the context)
> **All (of) the** equipment needs replacing. (specific equipment in the plant or other location)
> **All** equipment is dangerous. (all equipment in the world)

C. *Uses*

1. **Much** and **many** are more formal than **a lot of** and **lots of**:
    - Many of the employees feel very strongly about this issue.
    - A lot of the employees feel very strongly about this issue.

    How much and **how many** are the question words to ask about quantity:
    - How much have you budgeted for your new advertising campaign? (how much = money)

3. **Every** compounds:
    - I met everyone/everybody that I intended to. (*not:* all people what)
    - We did everything that was in the plan. (*not:* everything what)
    - They searched everywhere in Europe for a suitable plant.
    - Every time (that) the chairman visits us, I feel we have to put on a good show. (*not:* every time when)
4. Expressions of definite frequency (see Unit 51)
    We can use **each** or **every** with single periods:
    - We check the pumps each/every hour/morning/afternoon/day/week/month/year
    We use **every** where the period includes a number:
    - We test the alarm every three hours. (*not:* each three hours)
    - Every four weeks I visit the Middle East. (*not:* each four weeks)

NOTES

1. After **every** and compounds, we often use a plural pronoun to avoid using 'he' or 'she':
    Every manager should try their hardest to motivate their team.
    Everyone indicated their acceptance by raising their hands.
2. We do not use **each** or **every** with a negative verb:
    Despite the crisis, none of the plants was/were closed. (*not:* each of the plants wasn't closed)
3. **Every day** (adverb) is written as two words; **everyday** (one word) is an adjective:
    I go over to the plant every day.
    Problems like these are an everyday occurrence.
4. **Everyone/everybody/everything** (pronouns) are written as one word; but *every one* (each single one) is written as two:
    I have contacted everyone to discuss this matter. (all the people)
    Every one of the participants has now given me their replies. (each single one of the participants)

See also
Unit 59 – Quantifiers with **all, many, much, several, (a) few, (a) little** and **no**
Unit 60 – **Both, either** and **neither**

UNIT 62
Numerals

A. Sample sentences

- We have two plants in the UK and one in France.
- Our next plan is to open another plant in France.
- Half of our workforce come from the surrounding villages.
- We expect to employ 5,000 workers by the end of the century.
- We review our suppliers twice a year – once in the spring and once in the autumn.

B. Form

We can divide numerals into:

cardinals
ordinals
fractions and decimals
frequency expressions

1. Cardinals

Here are some examples:

0	nought, zero (especially in mathematics and for temperatures), 'oh' (in telephone numbers), nil (in sports)
100	a/one hundred; 'We offer a/one hundred different products'
101	a/one hundred and one
1,000	a/one thousand; 'At present have a thousand employees' (*not:* one thousand of)
1,101	one thousand, one hundred and one
3,000	three thousand; 'Three thousand delegates attended the conference' (*not:* three thousands of delegates)
1,000,000	a/one million
1,000,000,000	a/one billion

2. Ordinals

Here are some examples:

1st	first; 'The first of April' (spoken)
2nd	second; 'This is the second complaint we have made'
3rd	third; 'Our third attempt to find a solution was successful'
4th	fourth, 'He is our fourth production manager in as many years'
21st	twenty-first; 'These products will take us into the twenty-first century'
100th	(one) hundredth; our (one) hundredth new customer

C. Uses

1. **At**, **in**, **on** and **by**:
   At + clock time:
   - at 6 o'clock

   On + days of the week:
   - on Monday
   - on Thursday afternoon

   In + parts of the day:
   - in the morning/afternoon/evening
     but: at night

   On + dates:
   - on 3 May (spoken: on the third of May)

   In + months and years:
   - in May
   - in 1992 (spoken: in nineteen ninety-two)

   By + a deadline:
   - The installation must be finished by 1 January. (at the latest)

     Note: in time = with sufficient time/with time to spare
     on time = punctually

2. **For** and **during**:
   - The negotiations lasted for three hours. (length of activity)

   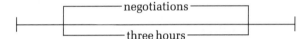

   - During the negotiations we had a short adjournment. (period within which another activity happened)

3. **Before** and **after**:
   - Before signature we must check the operation of the equipment
   - The guarantee period will start after signature of the contract.

4. Omission of time preposition:

   – before *this*, *last* and *next* when we use these words in relation to *now*:
   - this evening (*not:* in this evening)
   - last week
   - next time I go there

   – in phrases beginning with *yesterday* and *tomorrow*:
   - yesterday afternoon (*not:* in yesterday afternoon)
   - tomorrow morning

   – in expressions indicating the time frame:
   - I travel abroad 60 days a year. (*not:* in a year)
   - The train goes at 200 km an hour. (*not:* in an hour)

NOTES

1. **Last night** and **tonight**:

      Last night = the night of yesterday (*not:* yesterday night or this night)

      Tonight = the night of today (*not:* today night)

2. **The** before *previous*, *following*, *next* and *last* with *day* or parts of the day. We use **the** when we use the above words in time expressions not related to now:

      The previous evening = the evening before the one mentioned (*not:* in the previous evening)

      The following morning = the morning after the one mentioned (*not:* in the following morning)

      The next afternoon = the afternoon after the one mentioned

3. **Beginning, middle** and **end**:

      At the beginning of the meeting we discussed the agenda.

   but: 'In the beginning God created the heavens and the earth'

      We normally break for lunch in the middle of the day.

      I feel tired at the end of the day.

      In the end we got them to see our point of view. (finally)

4. **By** and **until/till.** We use **by** for an action which happens at or before a deadline:

      We must finish the construction by 1 January.

   We use **until** or **till** for an action which continues up to a deadline:

      We will continue working until/till 1 January.

5. **During** and **while. During** is a preposition; **while** is a subordinating conjunction (see Unit 43). Notice the parallel meanings in the following sentences:

      During his presentation he showed several interesting slides.

      While he was making his presentation he showed several interesting slides.

UNIT 64
Place

A. Sample sentences

- He has just left the office and gone into the plant.
- The raw material goes from the hopper here onto a conveyor belt there.
- Then the boards are stacked on this table here.
- Finally they are taken to the warehouse.

B. Form

We use a preposition before a noun or noun phrase:

> into the plant
> from the regional sales conference

We can divide prepositions of place into:

place prepositions
position prepositions
movement prepositions

1. Place prepositions

The preposition we use depends on our view of an object. The object may be:

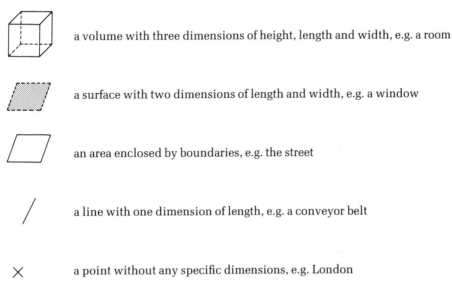

a volume with three dimensions of height, length and width, e.g. a room

a surface with two dimensions of length and width, e.g. a window

an area enclosed by boundaries, e.g. the street

a line with one dimension of length, e.g. a conveyor belt

a point without any specific dimensions, e.g. London

So, we have the following prepositions:

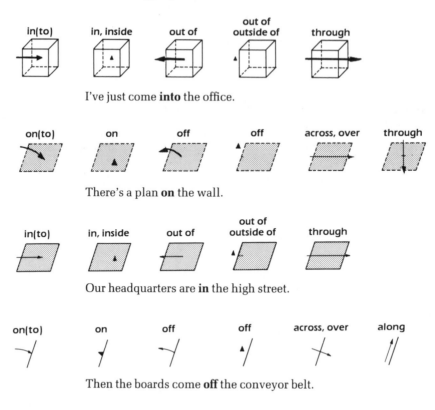

I've just come **into** the office.

There's a plan **on** the wall.

Our headquarters are **in** the high street.

Then the boards come **off** the conveyor belt.

We've been **at** the hotel since we arrived.

2. Position prepositions

These describe the relative positions of two objects. The main prepositions are:

above	**below**	**over**	**under**	**in front of**	**behind**
by	**beside**	**on top of**	**beneath**	**next to**	

The storage area is **next to** the production area.
The despatch area is **behind** the main building.

NOTES

Over/under and **above/below**
We normally use **over** and **under** to describe the direct vertical relationship:

If you look at the figures, you will see next year's forecast **under** this year's actual figures.

We use **above** and **below** to explain that one object is higher or lower than another:

> 300 metres **below** sea level
> 20 degrees **above** zero

3. Movement prepositions

The main prepositions are:

into	**out of**	**towards**	**away from**	**along**
behind	**in front of**	**across**	**over**	**onto**
up	**down**	**around**	**outside**	**through**

> The boards move **along** the conveyor belt.
> Then we put them **into** the corner.

C. Uses

In addition to the above rules, notice the following expressions.
1. With **at**:
    - At the top/bottom of the next page.
    - At the beginning/end of the contract.
    - At the front/back of the factory.
    - The plane arrived at the airport twenty minutes late. (arrive at a building)
    - *but:* We arrived in London just in time for our flight. (arrive in a country or city)
    - I'm sure he's still at work; he doesn't normally leave till after 6 o'clock. (also: at school/university)
    - He started work at 16. (or at the age of 16)
    - At last the computer system is working properly. (after a long time)
2. With **in**:
    - He is in the UK/in London. (with countries, towns and villages)
    - He is in prison for fraud. (he is a prisoner)
    - *cf.* He is at the prison. (he is visiting, i.e. not a prisoner)
    - He is in hospital/church/school/work.
    - He is in business/computers/plastics/medicine. (showing type of employment)
3. With **on**:
    - Take the first road on the left/right.
    - You'll find the secretary on the ground floor.
    - The letter is on top of my desk.
    - London is on the river Thames.
4. **In/into** versus **to**:
    - We drove in France. (inside France)
    - We drove into France. (we entered France from another country)
    - We drove to France. (France was our destination by car)
5. **To have been to**:
    - Have you ever been to the USA? (**have been** + **to** = to have gone and returned from, i.e. Have you ever visited . . . ?)

UNIT 65
Like *versus* as

A. Sample sentences
- As I said at the beginning of my presentation, sales have been very good. However, the situation has not been like last year.
- Before joining us he worked as sales manager for a pharmaceutical company.
- In my spare time I enjoy things like listening to music and reading.

B. Form
Both **like** and **as** are prepositions. **As** is also a subordinating conjunction (see Unit 36).

C. Uses
Both **as** and **like** mean 'the same as' or 'similar to'.
As:
- He works as a sales manager. (preposition; that is his real job)
- As I said before, this year's results are very encouraging. (conjunction; **as** + subject + verb; *not:* **like** + subject + verb)
- As mentioned earlier this evening, we have a guest speaker. (= as mentioned (by someone) earlier)
- The answers to the case study are as follows: first number 3, second number 2 and third number 1. (= as now to be told; *not:* as following)
- We use incentives, such as bonuses and merit awards. (for example)

Like:
- The plant is so hot that it is like an inferno. (it is not really an inferno)
- We use incentives like bonuses and merit awards. ('such as')
- I enjoy things like listening to music and reading. (*not:* 'to listen' because **like** is a preposition and is therefore followed by verb+**ing** – see Unit 12)
- It is not like them to keep us waiting for the deliver; they are usually very punctual. (notice the object pronoun after the preposition **like** – see Unit 56)

Like versus **as**:
- After the company reorganisation we started to operate as an independent division. (we *became* an independent division)
- After the company reorganisation we started to operate like an independent division. (but we did not actually become independent)

LANGUAGE

Part 2
Functions

UNIT 66
Classifying information

A. Sample sentences

- We can divide managers into first-line managers, middle managers and top managers.
- Managers can be classified as functional managers or general managers.
- There are four types of management activity: planning, leading, organising, and controlling.
- There are two parts to the process: mixing and filling.
- Managers fall into two classes: functional managers or general managers.

B. Form

We can classify information according to:
    its types
    its parts

1. The types

> We use two *types* of raw material.

Other nouns with the same meaning:

types   **sorts**   **varieties**   **kinds**

> We can *divide* managers *into* three classes.

Other verbs with similar meanings:

divide into   **classify as**   **split into**   **sort into**   **fall into**

2. The parts

> There are two *parts* to the process.

Other nouns with similar meanings:

parts   **elements**   **stages**   **steps**

> The process *consists of* a number of steps.

Other verbs with similar meanings:

consist of   **comprise**   **contain**   **involve**   **be divided into**
be broken down into   **be made up of**

C. Uses

1. Describing the types:

   - We can divide managerial roles into interpersonal, informational and decisional.
   - Managerial styles fall into a number of categories.
   - We can classify managers as planners, organisers, leaders and planners.

2. Describing the parts:

   - The tasks of first-line management consist of conceptual, human and technical activities.
   - Middle management's tasks also comprise conceptual, human and technical activities.
   - Top management are also involved in conceptual, human and technical activities.

NOTES

The department comprises six teams. (*not:* comprises of)

At the moment the department consists of six teams. (*not:* is consisting of)

UNIT 67
Connecting and sequencing ideas

A. Sample sentences

- *First* I'd like to look at total sales worldwide; *after that* we'll take a look at each region. *In particular*, I'd like to focus on the position in Europe. This will take up most of the morning. *So*, we'll need to change the timetable for the afternoon.

B. Form

Connectors and sequence markers are words or phrases which show the relationship between ideas, e.g. **first of all**, **therefore**, **in brief**. We put these words or phrases at or near the beginning of a sentence or clause. They connect subsequent information with earlier information:

> Sales have fallen, **therefore** we must intensify our marketing efforts. (cause)
> **However**, we must try to maintain the current level of marketing costs. (contrast)
> **After** seeing the experiences of other companies, we must take action to increase our market share. (time)
> **In brief**, we must increase the marketing effort while maintaining the current level of marketing costs. (summary of two main points)

We can use connectors and sequence markers to signal different types of relationship between ideas. The main relationships are:

time
logic (cause, contrast, condition, comparison, and concession – see Units 35 and 36)
text (addition, summary, paraphrase, example and highlight)

C. Uses

Below are the main words and phrases for the above relationships.
1. To signal time relationships

Beginning
> first/first of all/initially/to start with/the first step/at the first stage
> second/secondly/the second step/at the second stage
> third/thirdly/the third step/at the third stage, etc.
> then/after that
> next subsequently/the next step/at the next stage
> finally/the final step/at the final stage

End

Other language forms
Before + verb . . . *ing* (see Unit 12):
- Before going to the meeting, I read the report.

After + verb . . . *ing* (see Unit 12):
- After reading the report, I went to the meeting.

(After) having + verb . . . *ed*:
- (After) having read the report, I went to the meeting.

2. To signal logical relationships

   – *Cause:*

therefore	accordingly	consequently
as a consequence/result	hence (formal)	thus (formal)
because of this	that's why (informal)	so

   – *Contrast:*

yet	however	nevertheless	still
but	even so	all the same (informal)	

   – *Condition:*

   then   in that case

   – *Comparison:*

   similarly   in the same way

   – *Concession:*

   anyway   at any rate

   – *Contradiction:*

   in fact   actually   as a matter of fact   indeed

   – *Alternation:*

   instead   alternatively

3. To signal textual relationships

   – *Addition*:

also	in addition	moreover	furthermore
besides	too	overall	in brief/short

   – *Summary*:

   to sum up   then   overall   in brief/short

   – *Conclusion*:

   in conclusion   finally   lastly   to conclude

   – *Equivalence*:

   in other words   that means   namely   that is to say

   – *Inclusion*:

   for example   for instance   say   such as   as follows (written)
   e.g. (formal and written)

   – *Highlight*:

   in particular   in detail   especially   notably   chiefly   mainly

- *Generalisation*:

  usually   normally   as a rule   in general
  for the most part in most cases   on the whole

- *Stating the obvious*:

  obviously   naturally   of course   clearly

See also

Unit 34 – Sentence types – simple and complex
Unit 35 – Connecting ideas
Unit 36 – Subordinate clauses
Unit 37 – Equating and including ideas

UNIT 68
Describing trends

A. Sample sentences

- Energy costs have risen in line with inflation.
- Raw material costs have fallen slighly over the last year.
- We have had to put up our prices twice this year.
- We hope to see a moderate fall in overheads next year.

B. Form

Trends are changes or movements. These changes are normally in numerical items, e.g. costs, production volumes or unemployment. There are three basic trends:

For each trend there are a number of verbs and nouns to express the movement. We can divide the verbs into *transitive* and *intransitive*. After a transitive verb we must put an object:

We have raised **our prices** in line with inflation

After an intransitive verb we cannot put a direct object.

Our prices have risen in line with inflation.

1. ↗

Verbs		Nouns
Transitive	Intransitive	
increase	increase	increase
raise	rise	rise
put/push/step up	go/be up	
	grow	growth
extend		extension
expand	expand	expansion
	boom	boom (dramatic rise)

2. ↘

Verbs		Nouns
Transitive	Intransitive	
decrease	decrease	decrease
	fall	fall
drop	drop	drop
put/push down	go/be down	
	decline	decline
cut		cut
reduce		reduction
	collapse	collapse (dramatic fall)
	slump	slump (dramatic fall)

3. →

Verbs		Nouns
Transitive	Intransitive	
keep/hold . . . stable/constant	remain stable	stability
maintain . . . (at the same level)	stay constant	

4. Other expressions

To stand at. We use this phrase to focus on a particular point, before we mention the trends of movements:

In the first year sales in our region **stood at** 109,000 units

To reach a peak of:

In the sixth year sales in our region **reached a peak of** 24,000 units

Trends are changes. Sometimes we need to give more information about the change, as follows:

Raw material cost have fallen *slightly*. (the degree of change)

There has been a *rapid* increase in our expenses. (the speed of change)

Now let's look at this language in more detail. Remember that we modify a noun with an adjective (a *dramatic* rise); and a verb with an adverb (to rise *dramatically*)

5. Describing the degree of change

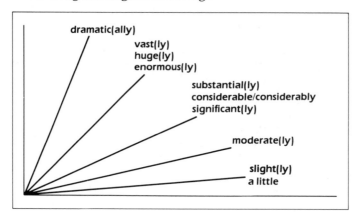

6. Describing the speed of change

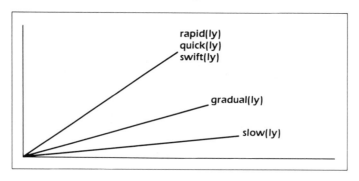

7. Showing changes

Notice
    a.   the different types of line we can use in a graph:

        —————   a solid line
        – – – –   a broken line
        ·············   a dotted line

    b.   the names for the axes on a graph:

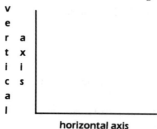

The vertical axis is also called the *y* axis and the horizontal axis the *x* axis.

c.   The different types of graphics:

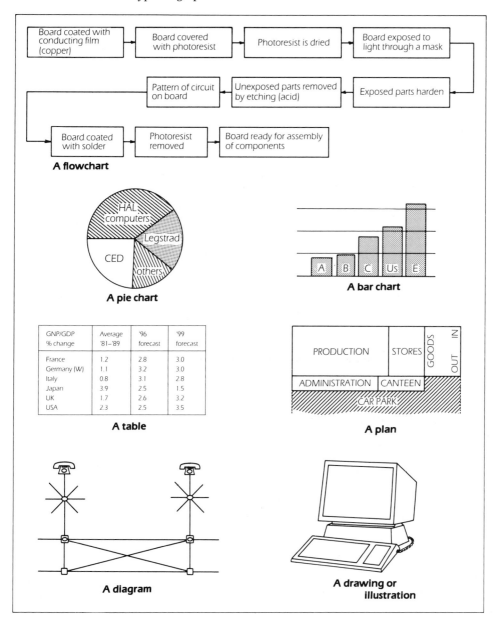

A flowchart

A pie chart

A bar chart

A table

GNP/GDP % change	Average '81–'89	'96 forecast	'99 forecast
France	1.2	2.8	3.0
Germany (W)	1.1	3.2	3.0
Italy	0.8	3.1	2.8
Japan	3.9	2.5	1.5
UK	1.7	2.6	3.2
USA	2.3	2.5	3.5

A plan

A diagram

A drawing or illustration

C. Uses

We can describe a trend by looking at:

- the difference between two levels
- the end point

1. Describing the difference:
   - This year sales have increased *by* 10 per cent (the difference between this year and last year is 10 per cent)
   - This year there has been an increase in sales *of* 10 per cent.

   Notice the prepositions. We use 'to increase *by*' (with the verb) and 'an increase *of*' (with the noun).

2. Describing the end point:
   - This year profits have risen to $2m. (the end result is that profits are up to $2m).
   - This year there has been a rise in profits to $2m.

   Notice the prepositions. We use 'to rise *to*' (with the verb) and 'a rise *to*' (with the noun).

NOTES

1. **Rise** and **raise**. For the use of the verbs, see Unit 27. Note the following use of the nouns with the meaning 'increase in pay':

   > We review wages in October and introduce the annual rise in January. (Br.E.)
   > We review wages in October and introduce the annual raise in January. (Am.E.)

2. Do not use **up** after 'increase', 'raise' and 'rise'; do not use **down** after 'fall', 'drop' and 'decrease':

   > We have raised our prices. (*not:* raised up)
   > Production volumes have fallen. (*not:* fallen down)

See also
Unit 49 – Adjective modification with adverbs
Unit 50 – Comparison of adjectives

UNIT 72
Comparing and contrasting ideas

A. *Sample sentences*
- Though local advertising is effective for supervisory posts, for middle and senior management we recommend national advertising.
- Top managers, in contrast to supervisory managers, need well-developed conceptual skills.
- Managers' tasks vary according to their position in the hierarchy.
- My present job responsibilities are very different from my previous ones.

B. *Form and uses*
We can use the following language techniques to compare and contrast ideas:

1. *Clauses of contrast (see Unit 40)*
These consist of two clauses: the main clause and the contrast clause:

┌──── Main clause ────┐ ┌──── Contrast clause ────┐
We will use their services *although* they are expensive.

The main conjunctions of contrast are:

but
though   *although*   *even though*
while   *whereas*

Notice the difference in use between **but** and the others:
- Local advertising is cheap but national advertising is more effective.
- Although local advertising is cheap, it is not as effective as national advertising.

2. *Phrases of contrast*
These consist of one clause which contains a phrase of contrast:

┌──────── Clause ────────┐
       ┌ Phrase of contrast ┐
We will use their services *despite* the high cost.

The main words to introduce a phrase of contrast are:

despite   *in spite of*   *notwithstanding* (formal)

- *Despite/In spite of* the skill shortage, we have managed to recruit workers without difficulty.

Notice the similar meanings of the following sentences:
- *Despite the poor economic climate*, our sales have held up. (phrase of contrast)
- *Although we are facing a poor economic climate*, our sales have held up. (clause of contrast)

3. Sentence connectors of contrast (see Unit 67)

These are words or expressions which link two sentences together which are in contrast to each other:

We have increased sales. *However*, our performance is not on target yet.

The main sentence connectors are:

yet   'however   nevertheless   still   but   even so   all the same (informal)

Notice the similar meanings of the following sentences:
- *Despite the reduction in our prices*, sales are still down. (phrase)
- *Even though we have reduced our prices*, sales are still down. (clause)
- We have reduced our prices. *Yet*, sales are still down. (sentence connector)

4. Clauses of comparison

These consist of one or two clauses:

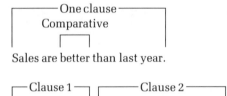

Sales are better than last year.

┌─Clause 1─┐ ┌─────Clause 2─────┐
Sales are better   than they were last year.

We can form clauses of comparison with the following language forms:
A comparative word + **than**
- Costs are rising *more quickly than* they have ever done.
- Losing a customer is always *easier than gaining* one. (notice the verb . . . *ing* after the preposition **than** – see Unit 12)
- Last year they sold *more than us*. (notice the object form after the preposition **than** – see Unit 56)

Rather than
- They should license the product *rather than sell* the invention. (Here **than** is a conjunction and therefore the verb *sell* takes the same form as *license*, i.e. infinitive with **to** – see Unit 34 note 3.)
- A: The chairman has just received the bad news. I've got to see him right away.
  B: Rather you *than me*! (= I'm glad that it is you rather than me – usually said about an unpleasant task or situation)

as . . . as and **not so . . . as**

- We have contacted *as many customers as* I intended.
- Even after streamlining our production, we are not *as/so profitable as them.* (notice the object form after the preposition **as** – see Unit 65)
- Selling to them is *as difficult as selling* ice to the Eskimoes. (notice the verb . . . *ing* after the preposition **as** – see Unit 12)

5. *Expressions of comparison and contrast*

in comparison with   compared to/with   in contrast with/to

- Their new product line is very sophisticated *in comparison with* ours.
- *In contrast with/to* previous years' results, these figures are very encouraging.

6. *Words and expressions of similarity and difference*

Note the following common expressions:

the same as   different from   similar to

- Even after streamlining the production we are facing *the same* problems *as* them. (*not:* the same like)

Verbs of similarity:

conform to   match   resemble   look like   correspond to

- All our products *conform to* standard European safety requirements.
- The new model *resembles* the AZ200 in appearance only, as the technology has been totally changed.

Verbs of difference (with the preposition **from**):

differ   vary   diverge   deviate

The new AZ200 *differs from* the AZ100 in two important respects.

See also
Unit 40 – Clauses of contrast
Unit 50 – Comparison of adjectives
Unit 67 – Connecting and sequencing ideas

UNIT 73
Checking and confirming information

A. Sample sentences

- Could you tell us when exactly the new model will be launched?
- What is the precise function of the new database?
- Don't you think that we could achieve our objectives by providing a better level of customer support?
- Let me just go over the main points again. Firstly, . . .

B. Form and uses

In the flow of communication, the speaker and the listener may need the following techniques for handling information:

asking for repetition
asking for clarification
asking for verification
asking for spelling
repeating information
correcting information

Below are some sentences that you can use.

1. Asking for repetition
   You may need to ask for repetition in two situations: if you didn't hear what was said or if you didn't understand what was said.

   − If you didn't hear, you can use one of these phrases:

   Sorry. (with a rising intonation)
   Pardon. (with a rising intonation)
   Pardon me. (with a rising intonation) (Am.E.)
   Excuse me. (with a rising intonation) (Am.E.)

   Another strategy is to state your problem and then make a request:

   (I'm) sorry I didn't hear what you said. ⎫
          I didn't quite catch what you said. ⎪ Stating your problem
          I didn't quite catch that. ⎬
          I missed that last part. ⎭

   Could you repeat what you said, please? ⎫
   Could you repeat that/say that again, please? ⎬ Making your request
   Would you mind repeating that, please? ⎭

NOTES

1. Notice the use of the positive and negative of **think**:
    > I think we should invest in a new computer system. (positive)
    > I don't think we should invest. (negative; *not:* I think we shouldn't invest)
    > I think so. (positive)
    > I don't think so. (negative)
2. **Think** versus **mean**
    > What do you think about the new model? (= what is your opinion)
    > What do you mean? (= what do you want to say?)
3. Other expressions to give opinions:
    > *As far as I am concerned*, we should introduce the new security arrangements as soon as possible.
    > *According to* the MD, the money is not yet available for the new system. (*not:* according to the MD's opinion)

See also

Unit 70 – Asserting and toning down information

Unit 76 – Agreeing and disagreeing

UNIT 76
Agreeing and disagreeing

A. Sample sentences

- I have talked to the foremen and they completely agree with the idea to set up a quality circle.
- We are in agreement over the payment terms; now we need to discuss the timing.
- I agree with Peter to a certain extent, but I still feel that we are exposing ourselves to unnecessary risks.
- I'm afraid we can't agree to the terms in your latest offer. Please reconsider them and get back to us.
- A productivity bonus for the workers? I totally disagree with that type of incentive.

B. Form and uses

We can use the following scale to show the range from *agreement* to *partial agreement* to *disagreement*.

We can also distinguish between agreeing with someone and agreeing to something

	Agreeing with someone	Agreeing to something
agreement	I totally agree with you I fully/completely agree I'm in total agreement with you there	I totally accept that I fully/completely agree I'm all in favour of that
partial agreement	Up to a point/To a certain extent I'd agree with you, but . . . You may have something there, but . . . You could/may be right, but . . .	Up to a point/To a certain extent I'd accept that, but . . . That may be so, but . . . That may/might be right, but . . .
disagreement	(I'm afraid) I can't agree with you I don't agree I can't go along with you on that	(I'm afraid) I can't accept that I don't accept that I can't go along with that

NOTES

1. **Agree** and **accept**

> I agree with you. (with someone; *not:* I am agree with you)
> I agree with the chairman's statement. (with something; = I have the same opinion as)
> I agree with you about/on the new plans. (= to share the same opinion about/on something)
> I agree to your request to postpone payment. (agree to something = to be willing to accept or allow something)
> I agree to review your credit position in a few months. (agree to do something; *not:* accept to do something)
> I accept your invitation. (to accept something; *not:* to agree something)

See also
Unit 75 – Asking for and giving opinions

UNIT 77
Cause and effect

A. Sample sentences

- The recent rise in interest rates has led to the bankruptcy of many small companies.
- Due to the recent rise in interest rates, many small companies have had to ask the banks to extend their overdrafts.
- The government is going to increase interest rates. As a result we will face short-term liquidity problems.

B. Form and uses

We can express the relationship between a cause and an effect in a number of ways. If we represent the relationship diagrammatically, we can see the link between the different language forms.

1. Verbs and verb phrases

We can view the relationship in two directions:

The recent rise in interest rates **has led to** bankruptcies.

A   = the cause
→   = the verb linking the cause to the effect
B   = the effect

Other verbs and verb phrases with a similar meaning are:

lead to	*result in*	*bring about*
give rise to	*account for*	*be responsible for*

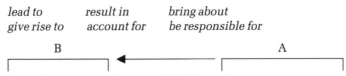

Many bankruptcies **have resulted from** the rise in interest rates

The symbols A and B have the same meaning:

←   = the verb leading the effect to the cause

Here are other verbs and verb phrases with a similar meaning

arise from	*stem from*	*be attributable to*

2. Clauses of cause (see also Unit 41)

Here a subordinating conjunction links the effect and the cause:

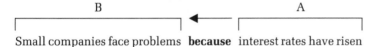

Small companies face problems **because** interest rates have risen

The other main subordinating conjunctions are:
because   *as*   *since*

3. Phrases of cause

Here an adverb phrase introduces the cause:

Due to low interest rates small companies can now invest

Other expressions with a similar meaning are

because of   *due to*   *owing to*
on account of *as a consequence of*

We always put a noun phrase after these expressions:
>Because of low interest rates, small companies are stronger. (*not*: because of interest rates are low)

4. Sentence connectors of cause

Here a cause in one sentence is linked to an effect in the following sentence by a connector.

Interest rates are up again. **Therefore,** we will face cash problems

The connector points backwards to the cause and forwards to the effect. Other connecting words and expressions are:

therefore   *accordingly*   *consequently*
so   *hence* (formal)   *thus* (formal)
as a consequence/   *that's (the reason)*   *why* (informal)
   result
because of this

See also
Unit 41 – Clauses of cause or reason

UNIT 78
Obligations and requirements

A. *Sample sentences*

- This year we really must try to reduce our costs.
- You have to have a sense of humour to work here – the wages are a joke.
- The new flexitime system doesn't require us to be in the office until core time starts at 10 o'clock, but we mustn't do less than 154 hours in a four-week period.
- I'm afraid the regulations forbid unauthorised visits to the plant.

B. *Form*

We can view the notion of obligation under the following headings:

> obligation to do something
> obligation not to do something, i.e. prohibition
> no obligation

We can also view the notion from the point of view of the person/situation causing the obligation (*the obliger*), and the person receiving the obligation (*the obliged*). First let's look at the range of verbs for the obliger:

Oblige s.o. to do s.th.	Oblige s.o. not to do s.th.	Not oblige s.o. to do s.th.
require	prohibit	not require
force	forbid	not force
compel	ban	not compel
make		not make
demand		
oblige		

Now let's look at the range of verbs for the obliged:

Obliged to do s.th.	Obliged not to do s.th.	Not obliged
must	mustn't	needn't
have to	not be allowed to	not have to
need to	not be permitted to	don't need to
be required to	be prohibited from	
be supposed to	may not	
be forced to	can't	

C. Uses

1. To oblige someone to do something:
   - The new regulations require workers to wear protective clothing in this area. (require/force/compel/oblige someone to do something)
   - The finance director now makes us prepare regular budgets. (*not:* make someone to do something)
   - The shareholders have demanded that we call an extraordinary meeting to discuss the present situation. (demand that someone does something)
2. To oblige someone not to do something:
   - The new regulations prohibit us from doing more than 10 hours overtime in any four-week period. (prohibit/forbid/ban someone from doing something)
3. Not to oblige someone to do something:
   - So far the company hasn't forced us to sign the new contracts of service.
   - They've asked for a refund, but they haven't made us take back the delivery.
4. To be obliged to do something:
   - We must take some radical measures to protect the company. (must do something)
   - Do you have to accept his word? Can't you consult someone else? (have to do something)
   - All companies are required to provide each employee with a contract of service. (to be required to do something)

NOTE

Often **must** and **have to** have the same meaning. Sometimes we use **must** for an 'internal' obligation – something that the speaker feels is necessary – and **have to** for an 'external' obligation – imposed from outside. Compare the following sentences:

We must take radical measures. (we feel they are necessary)
We have to take radical measures. (others feel they are necessary)

5. To be obliged not to do something:
   Companies mustn't/can't/may not start trading until they have registered their activities. (modal + infinitive without **to**)
   A company is not allowed/permitted to continue trading once the receiver has been called in. (not allowed/permitted to do something)
   He is prohibited from dealing on the Stock Exchange after his recent conviction for insider dealing. (prohibited from doing something)
6. Not obliged:
   You needn't accept the goods if you aren't satisfied. (needn't do something)
   Managers don't have to/need to have any formal qualifications. (don't have to/ need to do something)

See also
Unit 19 – **Must, mustn't** and **needn't**

UNIT 79
Ability and inability

A. Sample sentences
- We are pleased to inform you that we can make the funds available at the beginning of next week.
- Lower interest rates enable banks to offer cheaper money.
- We regret to inform you that we are unable to change the terms of the contract once it has been signed by both parties.
- Good managers should be capable of leading as well as managing.

B. Form
We can view the concepts of ability and inability in terms of:

making someone able or something possible:
>> The new rules **enable me to buy** equipment.
being able:
>> As a result **I can buy** equipment.
making someone unable or something impossible:
>> The new rules **prevent me from providing** credit.
being unable:
>> Therefore I **can't provide** credit.

Make able/ possible	Be able	Make unable/ impossible	Be unable
enable	can	prohibit	can't
allow	able to	prevent	not able/unable to
permit	capable of	stop	incapable of

C. Uses
1. Making someone able or something possible:
   - The terms of the contract allow us to reject deliveries which are more than 7 days late. (i.e. + object; *not:* allow/permit/enable to do)
2. Being able:
   - John can sign cheques on behalf of the company. (= normal ability)
   - John is able to sign cheques on behalf of the company (=exceptional ability, i.e. it is unusual or surprising that he can do it)
   - Good managers should be capable of leading as well as managing. (capable of verb . . . *ing*)

3. Making someone unable or something impossible:
   - This is the second time that he has stopped us from holding a meeting. (stop/prevent/prohibit someone from doing something or stop/prevent/prohibit something from happening)
4. Being unable:
   - I'd like to stay for the presentation, but I can't. (= something prevents me)
   - I'd like to stay for the presentation, but I'm unable to. (= something exceptional prevents me)
   - He is just incapable of consulting others. (incapable of verb . . . *ing*)

NOTE

He can speak English very well. (*not:* he can English very well)
He knows how to do it. (*not: he can it*)

See also
Unit 18 – **Can** and **could**

UNIT 80
Scale of likelihood

A. Sample sentences

- The recession is bound to lead to many bankruptcies.
- We are not likely to appoint a replacement for Mr Gilham.
- Inflation is already going down; the trading situation may improve quite rapidly.
- We can't possibly get anyone out to the terminal before next week.

B. Form

If we consider that the scale of likelihood goes from 100 per cent certainty to 0 per cent certainty, we can identify the following segments. (The numbers below are only a general indication, not exact values.)

certainty   (100%)   improbability   (25%)
probability   (75%)   impossibility   (0%)
possibility   (50%)

Certainty	I am **(absolutely) sure** / **certain** / **positive** } **that** sales will increase Sales will **definitely/certainly** increase Sales are **certain** / **sure** / **bound** } **to** increase
Probability	It is **(very) likely/probable that** sales will increase Sales are **(quite) likely to** increase Sales **should** increase
Possibility	Sales **may** increase Sales **might** increase
Improbability	It is **(very/highly)** { **unlikely that** sales will increase / **improbable** Sales are **unlikely to** increase
Impossibility	I am **sure** / **certain** / **positive** } **that** sales **won't** increase Sales **definitely/certainly won't** increase Sales **can't (possibly)** increase

Introduction

A definition

> **Communication** is the process of **transferring ideas or thoughts from one person to another** for the purpose of **creating understanding in the thinking** of the person receiving the communication.

Principles of effective communication

1. Establish the true **purpose** (instruction, persuasion, amusement, etc.)
2. **Clarify** your ideas before communicating
3. Be aware of prevailing **factors** (time, place, mood, etc.)
4. Determine the **method** (oral or written) and **channel** (e.g. phone, letter, presentation or meeting)
5. Make the communication **effective** and **unbiased**
6. Transmit the message **concisely** (short and clear)
7. Make sure there is **feedback**
8. Be a good **listener**
9. **Follow-up** the effect
10. Make sure the **right information**
    reaches the **right people**
        in the **right form**
            at the **right time**

SKILL 1
Presentations

Background

A presentation is a prepared talk given by a speaker (the *transmitter*) to one or more listeners (the *receivers*). To be effective, the speaker's message must pass to the listeners – it must be heard and correctly understood. In general, two-way communication is more effective than one-way communication; so, encourage the audience to provide feedback – by asking questions or making comments. In any case, remember that the talk is given for their benefit – not for the speaker's.

So, what are the elements of an effective presentation?

1.   The effective organisation of the information
2.   The effective delivery of the information
3.   The effective use of language

And, two final points:

4.   Never forget your audience
5.   Let them give feedback by questions or comments

Now let's expand points 1–3 to identify the skills and techniques you need.

1.   *Organisation of information*

   a.   Transparency of structure (have a clear beginning, middle and end)
   b.   Organisation of content (identify clearly main points and supporting points)
   c.   Level of information (start in the audience's area of interest)

2.   *Delivery of information*

   a.   Image (do you want to appear formal or informal, relaxed or high-powered?)
   b.   Audience features (what are their interests? how do they feel?)
   c.   Non-linguistic techniques (think about suitable body movements and eye contact)
   d.   Linguistic techniques (consider the use of short and long sentences, loud and quiet voice, silence, questions and humour)
   e.   Technical support (consider the use of aids, e.g. slides, diagrams on a flipchart and transparencies)

3.   *Use of language*

   a.   Vocabulary (choose the right word in spoken rather than written language)
   b.   Grammar (assemble the sentences correctly in terms of language forms)
   c.   Pronunciation (stress words and sentences correctly)
   d.   Fluency (vary your sentence structure; vary your sentence length)
   e.   Link your ideas, and don't talk too quickly

Pre-preparation

1. **Think about your objectives**
   a. What will be the change you wish to bring about in your audience?
   b. Do you want to inform them, amuse them, persuade them or train them? Or a combination of these?
2. **Think about the audience**
   a. What type of people are they?
   b. How many will there be?
   c. What mood will they be in?
   d. What is their level of knowledge on the subject?
   e. What is their level of understanding of English?
3. **Think about the time**
   a. How much time do you need for your presentation?
   b. How much time does the audience have for your presentation?
   c. How long can they concentrate?
   d. Then balance the equation.
4. **Think about the location**
   a. Will you be on a platform, in an office or in a conference room?
   b. How far will you be from the audience?
   c. Will you need to raise your voice?
   d. Will you need to use a microphone?
   e. Do you plan to use visual aids? Will all the equipment be there? Who will operate it?
5. **Think about your budget – especially in terms of time**
   a. How much time do you need to spend on preparing your talk and visual aids?

Planning your presentation

A quick checklist:
1. Why do you want to speak to this audience?
2. What will they expect to get out of it?
3. What main points do you want to make?
4. What is the best order to present them in?
5. What sort of relationship do you wish to establish with your audience?
6. How would you like/expect them to react?

Preparing your presentation

Five easy steps

1. **Collect** your material/ideas, jotting them down as they come to you on a piece of paper or a board. Be as wide-ranging as possible.
2. **Select** the points which seem most relevant for the situation you have defined.
3. **Group** the points which have some common thread, each group having a rough heading for the moment ('historical background', 'features of the product', 'practical problems', etc.).
4. **Sequence** these groups into an order which will make most sense for the audience.
5. Consider ways of **linking** the groups together, by a common idea, an analogy, a visual. The *language* for connecting and sequencing information is given in Unit 67.

Making and using notes

1. Consider placing your groups of information as headings arranged horizontally on the page, with the points listed vertically underneath. If the points are arranged in order of importance, this will allow omissions from the bottom of each column if time is short.
2. Make a note on the plan of the position of any audio-visual material, planned asides, anecdotes or questions. Use different symbols or colours.
3. Prepare any recordings or visual materials: overhead projection (OHP) transparencies, flipcharts, slides, samples. Make sure that visuals *are visual*, arrange them in such a way as to have visual impact.
4. Make a list of all the practical requirements (machinery, pens, number of sockets) you will have on the day, and make sure these are known by your host.
5. Decide what kind of notes you are going to work from on the day: none, headings, key phrases or substantial chunks.
   Use as few as possible. Use large writing, underlining and colours where suitable.

The introduction

1. Prepare your introduction. Include at least four pieces of information:
   a. What you're going to talk about
   b. How long you'll take
   c. What your main groups or sections are
   d. Whether you'd welcome questions during your talk, or only at the end.
   This could take as little as 45 seconds, but it will give you time to establish contact with the audience. This is when they are at their most receptive, so don't only impress them by your organisation and obvious preparation, go out of your way to make some comment on the present situation (excellent lunch, weather, lack of time – anything which shows awareness of the world outside your subject). Beware of jokes, but make as much eye contact as possible. If necessary, give a few facts about yourself and the purpose or background of your talk.

2. When your talk is ready, practise speaking it into a tape recorder and listen to yourself.

On the day

1. Make sure all the facilities you require are available and ready: machinery, materials and notes. Then forget about them.
2. Brief your chairman/presenter about who you are, what you're going to talk about, how long you'll take, time for questions, etc. If s/he makes a mistake, refer to this later, light-heartedly, rather than straight away.
3. Assess the amount of room available for movement, change of posture, gesture. Consider the role of this, in view of your own style.
4. Have ready some final comment which will end on the right note, perhaps based on the immediate situation, such as weather, time, length of talk, quality of questions or what you yourself have learnt from your presentation.

Structuring your presentation

The classical model

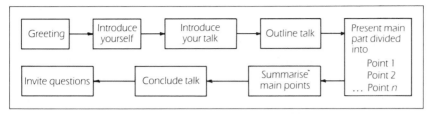

The introduction

Remember: First impressions count; so let the audience see your best qualities. In particular try to be:

Organised – make your plan of your talk 'transparent'.
Human – make some reference to the immediate situation, and relax.
Fluent – learn this part perfectly.
Brief – the audience have come for the *information*.

Here are some phrases you can use to introduce yourself and your talk:

- Good morning/afternoon/evening, ladies and gentlemen/colleagues. My name is . . . and I am marketing director of . . .

- I'd like to | say a few words to you today about the AZ120.
  | talk to you today about the AZ120.
  | explain to you today the operation of the AZ120.

- I shall take about 15 minutes of your time.
- I aim to talk to you for abour 15 minutes.
- This will take about half an hour.
- I've divided my talk into five main parts.
- The subject can be looked at under five main headings.
- During my talk I'll be looking at five main areas.

- If you have any questions, | please feel free to interrupt.
  | I'll be glad to try to answer them at end of my talk.

- To start with, then, I'd like to consider . . .

Linking ideas

It is vital to 'signal' to the audience what you are going to do and are about to do – to give a 'commentary' on your recent and planned progress, so that they know exactly where they are (and they know that you know).

You can choose from the list of linking sentences below. It is not complete, and will not suit the style of every speaker. Explore the full range, and, in the light of the subject of your talk, choose the ones that fit in best.

Explore alternative and less formal styles of 'commentary':

- The rhetorical question (That's the problem; what are the answers?)
- Displays of consideration (This part's quite hard/This isn't too obvious at first.)

LINKING SENTENCES

You can use the following sentences to link the different parts or sections of your presentation. Remember that they also give a clear 'signal' to your listeners as to the point you have reached in the structure of your presentation.

Introducing your first point
- To start with, then, I'd like to consider . . .
- First of all, I'd like to look at . . .

Finishing a point
- Those are the main points on . . .
- That's all I have to say about . . .
- So that, then, is . . .
- Now we've looked at/dealt with . . .

Starting a new point
- Now let's $\begin{cases} \text{turn to . . .} \\ \text{move on to . . .} \end{cases}$
- I'd like now to $\begin{cases} \text{consider . . .} \\ \text{examine . . .} \end{cases}$
- Next we come to . . .
- Turning now to . . .
- Let's move on now to . . .
- The next point I'd like to make is . . .

Referring to what you have said
- As I said at the beginning . . .
- I told you a few moments ago that . . .
- In the first part of my talk, I said . . .
- As I've already said, . . .
- As I mentioned earlier, . . .

Referring to what you will say
- I'll come to that later.
- I'll return to this point in a few minutes.
- . . . and I'll talk about this in the next part of my presentation.
- . . . I'll comment on this in my conclusion.

Summarising
- So now I'd just like to summarise the main points.
- In brief, we have looked at . . .

Concluding

- That's all I have to say for now.
- (I think) that covers most of the points.
- That concludes my talk.
- Thank you for your attention.

Inviting questions

- And now, if you have any questions, I'll be glad to (try to) answer them.
- Does anyone have any questions?
- Any questions?

This section has dealt with linking sentences. You can find more about connecting words in Unit 67 – Connecting and sequencing ideas.

SKILL 2
Meetings

Background

Managers spend a lot of time in meetings. In fact many managers would argue 'too much time'. So, what exactly is a meeting in the management sense? Let us define it as:

> The **gathering together**
> of a **group of people**
> for a **controlled discussion**
> with a **specific purpose**

Having defined a meeting, the next question is: when should you call a meeting?

1. When decisions require judgement rather than calculation or expertise. (problem-solving)
2. When pooling ideas improves the chances of good decisions. (idea-generating)
3. If 'acceptance' of the decision is an important consideration for members.
4. To discuss multi-faceted problems requiring different skills or specialists.

So what are the essential elements of a meeting?

1. *A purpose.* The three basic purposes of meetings are problem-solving, idea-gathering or training.
2. *An agenda.* Without a list of points any meeting will quickly go out of control, and an uncontrolled meeting is most unlikely to be effective or efficient.
3. *Members.* There are three types:

    the chairman (or chairperson)
    the secretary
    the other participants

    All the members will be expected to prepare for the meeting, and, when there, to concentrate, communicate and co-operate in order to produce . . .
4. *A result:* the whole object of the exercise. However, this will be insufficient without . . .
5. *A report:* normally the minutes of the meeting.

What makes a good meeting?

We have looked at the essential elements of a meeting. But what makes a good meeting? What are the techniques and skills needed by the participants?

Firstly, we can distinguish between the chairing skills and participating skills. Secondly, we can distinguish between language skills and behavioural skills.

The following diagram shows the main elements:

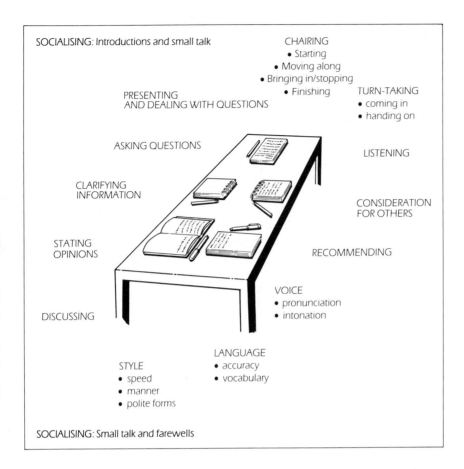

SOCIALISING: Introductions and small talk

CHAIRING
• Starting
• Moving along
• Bringing in/stopping
• Finishing

TURN-TAKING
• coming in
• handing on

PRESENTING
AND DEALING WITH QUESTIONS

ASKING QUESTIONS

LISTENING

CLARIFYING
INFORMATION

CONSIDERATION
FOR OTHERS

STATING
OPINIONS

RECOMMENDING

VOICE
• pronunciation
• intonation

DISCUSSING

LANGUAGE
• accuracy
• vocabulary

STYLE
• speed
• manner
• polite forms

SOCIALISING: Small talk and farewells

Chairing a meeting

The chairman must control the meeting so that it can reach a successful conclusion and achieve its purpose. Although the exact style of chairing will depend on the purpose and type of meeting, the diagram on the next page shows the main tasks that the chairman needs to perform.

Some meetings need a referee; some need a captain. But they all need someone to make sure that the maximum amount of business is conducted in the minimum amount of time. This is the role of chairman (addressed 'chairman', 'mister chairman' or 'madam chairman'), who needs a certain amount of language to get things started, keep them going and lead them to a conclusion. Here are some phrases you can use:

Opening the meeting

- Good morning, ladies and gentlemen/colleagues.

- If we are all here | shall we start/make a start/get started?
  let's start/make a start/get started?
  I think we should start/make a start/get started.

- First of all | I'd like to introduce | two colleagues from our Munich office.
  let me introduce

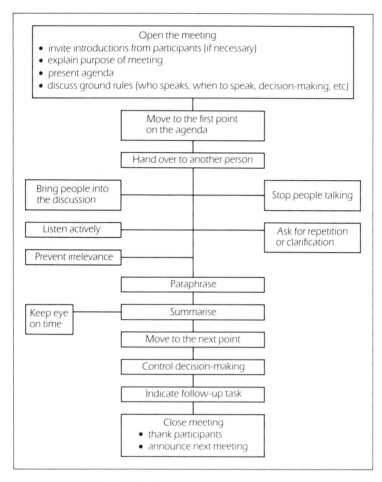

Open the meeting
- invite introductions from participants (if necessary)
- explain purpose of meeting
- present agenda
- discuss ground rules (who speaks, when to speak, decision-making, etc)

Move to the first point on the agenda

Hand over to another person

Bring people into the discussion — Stop people talking

Listen actively — Ask for repetition or clarification

Prevent irrelevance

Paraphrase

Keep eye on time — Summarise

Move to the next point

Control decision-making

Indicate follow-up task

Close meeting
- thank participants
- announce next meeting

- Would you like to say a few words about yourselves?
- Right, thank you.
- Have you all got a copy of the agenda?
- If everyone has got a copy of the agenda, let me first explain the purpose of the meeting.
- The objective/purpose/aim/target of this meeting is to . . .
- Now let's look at the agenda in detail.
- As you can see there five main points/items.
- I propose/suggest that we take them in the following order.
- I think we will need about 30 minutes for point/item 1, 20 minutes for point/item 2, ...
- As we have a lot to get through this morning, can we agree on the ground rules? I suggest/propose the following: . .

Moving to the first point
- Right. Now let's move on to/look at the first point.

Handing over to another person
- Right, Jeremy, over to you.

Bringing people in (encouraging hesitant speakers)
- We haven't heard from you yet, George. What do you think about this proposal?
- Would you like to add anything, Margaret?
- Anything to add, Peter?

Stopping people talking
- One at a time, please!
- We can't all speak at once. John first, then Mary, then Max.
- Would you mind addressing your remarks to the chair? (*but don't silence the person who talks too much; you may need him or her later*)
- Well, thank you, Deborah. I think that's clear now. Could we have some other opinions?
- Right, thank you, Peter. I think we've all got the point now. Shall we move on?
- Okay John, thanks. Susan, I think you wanted to say something?

Listening actively

What to do	What to say
Nod head	Right, I see
Lean forwards	Okay, I understand
Study the speaker	Um, that's interesting
Show interest	Right
Maintain eye contact	Okay

Asking for repetition or clarification
1. If you didn't hear, you can say:
   - (I'm) sorry. I didn't hear what you said. Would you mind repeating it, please?
2. If you didn't understand, you can say:
   - (I'm) sorry. I don't quite follow you. Could you go over that again, please?
3. If you feel the speaker is being vague or imprecise, you can say:
   - What exactly do you mean by . . . ?

For further expressions, see Unit 73 – Checking and confirming information

Preventing irrelevance
- I'm afraid that's outside the scope of this meeting.
- We're beginning to lose sight of the main point.
- Keep to the point, please.
- I think we'd better leave that subject for another meeting.

Paraphrase
- So what you're saying is . . .
- In other words . . .
- So you mean . . .
- So, if I understand you correctly . . .

Summarising
- To sum up then, . . .
- So, to summarise what has been said so far, . . .

Keeping an eye on the time
- We're running short of time.
- There's not much time left. | Could you please be brief?

Moving to the next point
- Right. Let's move on to the next point
- Geraldine, would you like to introduce the next point?
- Okay, on to item 4. Who's going to open this one?
- Well, I think that covers everything on that point. Let's move on.

Controlling decision-making
- I'd like to (formally) propose that . . .
- I'd like to propose the following amendment.
- Can we take a vote on that proposal?
- All those in favour. Right. All those against. Right, thank you.
- So that motion has been accepted/rejected by 4 votes to 3.
- Very well, then, we agree with some reservations/unanimously that . . .
- Well, it seems that we are broadly in agreement that . . .

Indicating follow-up tasks
- Paul, do you think you could . . . ?
- Derek, how about preparing some figures for the next meeting?

Closing the meeting
- Right. That just about covers everything.
- I'd like to thank Marianne and Anke for coming over from Munich.
- So, the next meeting will be on . . . (date) at . . . (time)
- Thanks for your participation
- Right, I declare the meeting closed.

Participating in a meeting

After you have got the chair's attention and been given the floor, the range of language that you may wish to express is very wide. Below is a list of some typical functions that you may need. After each is the reference to the relevant unit in section A part 2 – Functions.

1. Getting the chair's attention

(Mister/Madam) Chairman,	may I come in here?
	I'd like to comment on that.
	may I have the floor for a moment?
	point of order!

2. Asking for and giving opinions – Unit 75.
3. Agreeing and disagreeing – Unit 76.
4. Advising and suggesting – Unit 81.
5. Requesting information and action – Unit 82.
6. Checking and confirming information – Unit 73.
7. Comparing and contrasting ideas – Unit 72.
8. Asserting and toning down information – Unit 70.
9. Connecting and sequencing ideas – Unit 67.
10. Describing trends – Unit 68.

Questioning techniques, style and language

This section deals with questioning – a key skill not only in meetings but also in other areas of business communication, e.g. interviewing, counselling, post-presentation questioning and phoning.

Techniques of questioning

1. Your question should have a definite purpose in mind.
2. State your question clearly, leaving no doubt as to what is required.
3. Your question should be neither so easy as to require little thought nor so difficult as to discourage effort.
4. Ask your question in a natural manner, indicating that you have confidence in the other person's ability to answer it.
5. Particularly in large gatherings, e.g. conferences, use open direct questions such as **wh**-questions, i.e. questions starting with 'who', 'what', 'where', 'when', 'why' or 'how' (see Unit 38 – Questions, and Unit 82 – Requesting information and action).
6. After asking your question, wait for an answer; don't answer your own questions.
7. Take answers from one person at a time; don't interrupt.
8. Encourage complete and clearly expressed answers.
9. See that everyone has an equal opportunity to provide answers.

Types of question

1. Overhead	General questions to the whole group
2. Direct	Question to a specific individual
3. Factual	Asking for facts, data or information
4. Leading	Questions that suggest answers
5. Encouraging	Questions that help respondents
6. Ambiguous	Questions that suggest two or more answers

7.	Controversial	Questions that suggest two or more answers and are likely to lead to disagreement
8.	Provocative	Questions to incite people to answer
9.	Probing	Questions to check an individual's knowledge
10.	Closed	Questions with the answer 'yes' or 'no'
11.	Supportive	Questions which show that the questioner agrees with the respondent
12.	Redirected	Questions directed at the leader, but returned to the group

Examples of questions

1.	Overhead	What are the figures for the last quarter?
2.	Direct	Jeremy, what is the current budget?
3.	Factual	When will the system be installed?
4.	Leading	I suppose you are pretty busy?
5.	Encouraging	I'd be interested to hear about . . .
6.	Ambiguous	Is it a good move to make the investment now?
7.	Controversial	Are managers born or made?
8.	Provocative	What do you feel about the claim in the press that we have wasted the company's money?
9.	Probing	Could you give us an example of . . . ?
10.	Closed	Do you think we can solve this problem?
11.	Supportive	So you feel this is pretty important?
12.	Redirected	(Person A → person B)
		What exactly is 'globalisation'?
		(Person B → person A)
		John, how would you define 'globalisation'?

SKILL 3
Telephoning

Background

The telephone is very much an essential part of business life. It brings with it certain advantages for the users, but also certain disadvantages. Let's look at both sides of the coin.

Advantages

1. Immediate contact and feedback: the telephone enables people to communicate without a personal meeting
2. Economy of time and money
3. More personal than writing
4. If used well, creates a good image of reliability, efficiency and courtesy
5. Can create, affect and correct relationships
6. Demands and retains attention

Disadvantages

1. The receiver may be unprepared

2. No record of the conversation
3. No face-to-face contact
4. Creates a bad image if used badly or not used
5. If used badly, can damage relationships

6. The receiver may feel that the call is an intrusion

Having looked at the advantages and disadvantages of the telephone as a medium, the next question is: when should you use the phone?

1. When speed is important.
2. When no written record is needed.
3. When you are sure you can contact the right person.
4. When you are sure that your call can be effective.

So, what are the elements of an effective phone call?

1. Good practice: can you control the call and conduct it with politeness and efficiency? Do you consider and help the receiver?
2. Clear objectives: why are you making the call?
3. Relevant information: have you got all the necessary information to hand?
4. A clear strategy: do you have a plan of your tactics for the call?
5. An action plan: do you have a procedure for follow-up?

Structuring a call

Outgoing calls (i.e. when you make the call)

Greeting
- Good morning/afternoon/evening.
- Hello. (informal)

Identifying yourself
- My name is . . . (first introduction)
- This is . . . here. (second and subsequent introduction)
- This is . . . (speaking).

Asking to speak to someone
- Could I speak to . . . , please?
- Could you put me throught to . . . , please.
- Could I have extension 4356, please?
- I'd like to speak to . . . , please.
- John Brown, please.

Giving further details
- It's in connection with . . .
- It's about . . .

Explaining purpose of call
- I'm calling to ask about . . .
- I'm phoning to let you know the details of . . .
- I'm ringing to tell you about . . .

Showing understanding
- I see.
- I understand.
- Yes/Right/Fine/Okay.

Making an appointment
- Could we meet some time soon?
- When could we meet?
- When could I see you?
- What time would suit you?
- Would . . . (day) at . . . (time) suit you/be okay?
- Can you manage . . . (day) at . . . (time)?

Leaving a message
- Could you give . . . a message, please?
- Could you ask . . . to call me (when he gets back)?
- (Could you tell . . .) I'll call back later.

Confirming details

- Well, I look forward to | meeting you next week, then.
  receiving the contract by fax, then.
  hearing from you later today, then.

Thanking
- Well, thank you very much for your help.
- Well, thanks for the information.
- I'm much obliged to you.
- I'm very grateful for your assistance. (formal)
- Well, thanks a lot. (informal)

Ending the call
- I look forward to seeing/hearing from/meeting you.
- See you/speak to you soon. (informal)
- Goodbye/Bye.

Incoming calls (i.e. when you receive the call)

Identifying yourself when you pick up the phone
- Hilary Beacham.
- Hilary Beacham speaking.
- *Caller*: Could I speak to Hilary Beacham, please?
  Receiver: Yes, speaking.

Helping the caller
- Can I help you?
- Who would you like to speak to?

Asking for the caller's identification
- Who's speaking, please?
- Who's calling, please?
- And who would like to speak to her, please?
- And your name is?

Asking for further information
- What's it in connection with, please?

Explaining that someone is not available
- I'm afraid . . . is not available this morning/afternoon/at the moment.
- I'm afraid . . . is out/in a meeting/with a client at the moment.
- I'm sorry, but . . . is on holiday/not in the office today/this week.
- I'm sorry, but . . . is on the other line at present.
- I'm afraid his/her line's engaged. Do you want to hold?

Alternative actions
- Could you ring/call/phone back later?
- Would you like to leave a message?
- Can I take a message?

Confirming information
- Yes, that's right/correct.

Confirming arrangements
- Yes, | that suits me fine.
  | that would be fine.
  | that's fine.

Declining arrangements and suggesting alternatives
- I'm afraid I won't be in the office on . . . (day).
- I'm sorry, but . . . (day/time) doesn't suit me at all.
- I'm afraid I can't manage/make . . . (day/time).
- Can you manage . . . (day) at . . . (time)?
- I could make it on . . . (day) at . . . (time).
- How about . . . (day/time)?

Responding to thanks
- Not at all.
- Don't mention it.
- You're welcome.

Ending the call
- I look forward to seeing/hearing from/meeting you.
- See you/speak to you soon. (informal)
- Thanks for calling.
- Goodbye/Bye.

Telephone techniques

Improving your performance

1. **Stay in control of your emotions**

Tension leads to loss of concentration, and this leads to poor communication. Before you make a difficult call, relax your mind and muscles. Above all, **be polite** when dealing with others; **be firm** and avoid time-wasting; and when you've finished **be gone**.

2. **Stay in control of the call**

If you want to sound more authoritative, then stand up; if you want to sound more relaxed, then sit back in your chair.

3. **Stay in control of your language**

Remember that in a phone call both parties have to rely on their language skills; there is no supporting body language. So, when it's your turn:

- speak clearly and slowly
- avoid complex language
- don't repeat yourself
- use questions to identify issues and clarify points
- use cues to indicate when the other person should speak

When it's the other person's turn:
- don't interrupt
- don't impose your ideas
- don't answer your own questions
- and above all, take as long as you need, but keep your call as short as possible

4. **Overcome your fear of the phone**

Never talk 'at' the handset. Instead, imagine that the person you are calling is sitting opposite you. Speak to them directly. Picture their responses to your remarks. Use the same body language as you would if you were face-to-face. This will make your voice sound more relaxed, confident and natural.

5. Listen

Listening is not the same as hearing; effective listening means hearing + perceiving + understanding. Ineffective listening happens when you get distracted – thinking you can do two things efficiently at the same time; or when you are dismissive – not attending to the message, but thinking your own thoughts. Also, listen to the speaker's tone of voice. As you can't see the other person, you need to rely on tone to provide important clues to hidden meanings.

To improve your listening, choose the appropriate ear. To analyse complicated facts, listen through your right ear, as this communicates with the left – logical – side of the brain. To listen sympathetically, listen through your left ear, as this sends information to the right – intuitive and imaginative – side of the brain.

Dealing with problems

1. Dealing with language difficulties

If you can't hear or don't understand what the other person says, take action immediately. Appropriate language to ask for repetition or clarification is given in Unit 73.

2. Making difficult calls

a. Before ringing, decide exactly what you want to achieve from the call.
b. Check your facts carefully and have all the necessary evidence to hand.
c. Get quickly to the purpose of your call.
d. Be forceful and assertive until you get satisfaction.
e. Don't get personal or lose your temper.

3. Receiving difficult calls

a. Be a good listener and listen sympathetically.
b. Don't take personally complaints against the company.
c. Don't be aggressive; remain as calm and objective as possible.
d. Encourage the other person to voice all their complaints before starting to deal with them.
e. Restate their complaints in your own words to clarify the issues in your own mind and to get confirmation from the other person.
f. Don't offer to do what you are not authorised to do; don't agree to do anything until you have checked all the facts.

SKILL 4
Letter-writing

Background

Why write a letter when you can use the phone or meet face-to-face? There are a number of reasons for using the letter as the medium of communication. Most important are:

1. Letters can *formalise ideas*. A well written letter needs a clear structure; and a clear structure needs systematic and logical development. So, writing helps to clarify thoughts.
2. Letters can *simplify ideas*. The process of drafting a letter can reduce ideas to short, simple and essential information.
3. Letters *project an organisation's image* – through the logo, the writer's style and the appearance of the document.
4. Letters are *tangible*. They are a written record of a message transmitted by the writer. They are also a more permanent record than a phone call.
5. Letters are *cheaper*, especially when compared to long-distance phone calls.

In summary, we can say that a letter is the appropriate medium:

1. When immediate feedback isn't needed or isn't possible, e.g. when inviting comments on a proposal.
2. When personal contact isn't needed or isn't possible, e.g. when confirming an appointment made by phone.
3. When a written record is needed, either as a permanent record or as a symbol of the company's image, e.g. a proposal.
4. When you are not sure you can contact the right person by phone or the right person is difficult to get hold of.
5. When a large number of standard messages need to be transmitted, e.g. a mailshot.

So, what are the elements of effective letter-writing?

1. *Good practice:* the need for good physical presentation and layout.
2. *Clear objectives:* Why are you writing the letter? What has caused the letter to be written? What results do you want from the letter?
3. *The message:* the need for the right information in clear language and appropriate style.
4. *Anticipation of the likely result:* how do you expect the reader to react?
5. *An action plan:* do you have a procedure for follow-up?

Structuring a letter

Presentation and layout

Letters are important in creating a good impression. Therefore, *what* is written is as vital as *how* it is presented. There are various styles appropriate to business letters. These must take into account:

> the company's letterhead
> the company's inhouse writing style.

In addition, the style of letters is constantly changing in line with different international business practices and new language developments. However, a good business letter should aim to be:

precise
concise
accurate

The following are examples of five types of business letter.

A letter of application

63 Wenwell Gardens
Southtown
SO9 7PX

↑
The sender's address

Inventor Plus
20 Chiswick Avenue   ← *The addressee*
Southtown
SO3 6QZ

10 January 19— ← *The date*

The greeting (where the addressee's name is not known)

Dear Sir/Madam
                The first paragraph says why you are writing
I am writing in response to your advertisement for a Personal Assistant/Secretary to the Managing Director.   *The second paragraph gives further details*

I am enclosing a copy of my curriculum vitae, which gives details of my qualifications and experience. As you will see I have had 7 years' experience of working in a business environment and have an RSA 2 in Typing and Shorthand. Although I did not have to travel in my previous job, I would be very willing to do so.

I will be available for interview at any time, and look forward to hearing from you.

Yours faithfully *The farewell (after Dear Sir/Madam)*   *The final paragraph includes a polite ending*

Hilary Beacham ← *The signature*

Hilary Beacham   ← *The person writing the letter*

A letter of request

Softchain Ltd
(Head Office), Foss House, Brigham Street, Liverpool L13 4AT
Tel: 051-387 6397   Fax: 051-387 9284

The letterhead includes the name and address of the sender

Compact Systems
96 Rosewall Drive
Southtown
SO3 4BT   *← The addressee*

Your ref:
Our ref: Inq. B7693

↖ The sender's reference

5 April 19— *← The date*

The greeting (where the addressee's name is not known)

Dear Sirs   *The first paragraph says why you are writing*

We recently attended the Software Trade Exhibition in Bath, and were impressed by the range of software available through your company.

← The second paragraph gives the real reason for writing

We are a large chain of business software retailers and are looking for a software house which could supply us with a range of business applications programs.

As we usually place large orders, we would expect a quantity discount in addition to a 20 p.c. trade discount off net list prices. Our terms of payment are normally 30 days after receipt of invoice.

If these conditions are of interest to you, we would be much obliged if you could send us your current catalogue and price list.

The final paragraph is a polite ending

We look forward to hearing from you soon.

Yours faithfully *← The farewell (after Dear Sirs)*

pp. *Pat Miles.*   *← The signature*

P. Barker *←————— The person writing the letter*
Purchasing Manager *← The writer's position in the company*

pp. means that Pat Miles signed the letter for P. Barker

A letter of reply

—————————————— Compact Systems ——————————————

96 ROSEWALL DRIVE, SOUTHTOWN, SO3 4BT   TEL: 0927 423845   FAX: 0927 423617

Mr P. Barker   Your ref: Inq. B7693
Purchasing Manager   Our ref: AE/677
Softchain Ltd
Foss House   *The addressee's*
Brigham Street   *reference*
Liverpool
L13 4AT
                                      Alternative position for the date

                                      10 April——

Dear Mr Barker *The greeting (where the addressee's name is known)*

Thank you for your letter of 5 April 19—— in which you asked for details of our range
of business applications programs.

Because of the low price of our software we do not normally offer a quantity discount;
however, if you can give me an indication of the quantity involved, I would be happy
to discuss terms further with you. Normally, we would be happy to offer you a 20 p.c.
trade discount off net list prices, as requested in your letter, and to accept your terms
of payment.

I am enclosing a copy of our most recent catalogue, which gives details of your
product range, together with list prices. I hope that the information will be of
interest to you, and look forward to discussing orders in the near future.

Yours sincerely *The farewell (after a named addressee)*

pp. Hilary Beacham

Alice Everett
Marketing Manager   *The enclosed documents*

Encl. Compact catalogue, trade price list

        'Encl.' means enclosure(s)

A letter of order

Softchain Ltd
(Head Office), Foss House, Brigham Street, Liverpool L13 4AT
Tel: 051-387 6397   Fax: 051-387 9284

Mrs A. Everett   Your ref: AE/677
Compact Systems   Our ref: Ord. B7693
96 Rosewall Drive
Southtown
SO3 4BT

15 July 19—

Dear Mrs Everett

Please find enclosed our order, Ord. B7693, for 100 IBM-compatible Compact Accounts packages, as discussed in our phone conversation of 12 July.

We have decided to place an order for 100 packages and accept the 20 p.c. trade discount off net list prices as discussed. Payment will be made, as agreed, 30 days after receipt of your invoice.

We would be much obliged if you could despatch the goods so that they reach us no later than 30 July, and look forward to receiving your acknowledgement.

Yours sincerely

P. Barker

P. Barker
Purchasing Manager

Encl. Ord. B7693

A letter of complaint

Softchain Ltd
(Head Office), Foss House, Brigham Street, Liverpool L13 4AT
Tel: 051-387 6397   Fax: 051-387 9284

Mrs A. Everett   Your ref: AE/677
Compact Systems   Our ref: Ord. B7693
96 Rosewall Drive
Southtown
SO3 4BT

2 August 19––

Dear Mrs Everett

On 15 July we placed an order for 100 IBM-compatible Compact Accounts packages. A consignment was delivered on 30 July, but upon inspection we found that the packages were not IBM-compatible.

As this is our first transaction with your company we are naturally disappointed that we have got off to such a bad start. Therefore I would be much obliged if you could send us the correct goods as soon as possible, and arrange for the collection of the incorrect ones.

Yours sincerely

P. Barker

P. Barker
Purchasing Manager

Beginning and ending a letter

Opening a letter

To a:	British English	American English
company	Dear Sirs	Gentlemen
man (name unknown)	Dear Sir	Dear Sir
woman (name unknown)	Dear Madam	Dear Madam
person (name and sex unknown)	Dear Sir/Madam	Dear Sir/Madam
man	Dear Mr Bennett	Dear Mr. Bennett
woman (married or widowed)	Dear Mrs Bennett	Dear Mrs. Bennett
woman (unmarried)	Dear Miss Bennett	Dear Miss Bennett
	Dear Ms Bennett	Dear Ms. Bennett
woman (marital status unknown)	Dear Ms Bennett	Dear Ms. Bennett
married couple	Dear Mr and Mrs Bennett	Dear Mr. and Mrs. . . .
unmarried couple	Dear Mr Bennett and Mrs Black	Dear Mr. . . . and Mrs. . . .
friend or acquaintance	Dear Peter	Dear Peter

Closing a letter

The closing depends on the opening

If you start:	then close: British English American English
Dear Sirs/Sir/Madam	Yours faithfully
Gentlemen	Sincerely yours (Very) Truly yours
Dear Mr/Mrs/Miss/Ms Bennett (Br.E.)	Yours sincerely
Dear Mr./Mrs./Miss/Ms. Bennett (Am.E.)	Yours sincerely Sincerely yours (Very) Truly yours Yours (very) truly
Dear Peter	(With) Best wishes (Best) Regards

In British letters the closing is fixed by the opening; in American English the closing depends on the degree of formality.

1. Formal tone: Yours truly, Yours very truly, Very truly yours
2. More formal tone: Respectfully yours, Yours respectfully, Very respectfully yours, Yours very respectfully
3. More personal tone: Sincerely, Cordially, Sincerely yours, Cordially yours, Yours sincerely

Starting the letter

- Thank you for your letter of . . . (date)
- I have received your letter of . . . (date)

asking if/about . . .
concerning . . .
enclosing . . .
in which you asked . . .

Explaining purpose of letter

- We are writing to enquire about/whether . . .
- We are writing to ask about/if . . .
- I am writing in connection with . . .
- I am writing in response to . . .
- With reference to . . .
- Further to . . .
- With regard to . . .

Finishing the letter

- I look forward to meeting/hearing from you.
- Looking forward to meeting/hearing from you.
- We look forward to receiving the proposal/your order/your reply.

The main part

Requesting

- We would be very grateful if you could . . .
- I would be much obliged if you could . . .
- We would appreciate if you could . . .
- Please could you . . . (informal)

Giving information or replying to a request for information

Positive	*Negative*
- Please find enclosed . . .	We regret to inform you . . .
- We are happy to enclose . . .	We are sorry to tell you . . .
- We wish to inform you . . .	
- We are pleased to inform/advise you . . .	

Thanking

- I am much obliged to you for sending me . . .
- I am grateful to you for . . .
- We are much obliged to you for . . .
- Thank you for . . . (informal)

Apologising

- We were (very/extremely/most) sorry to hear about the problem.
- We regret that this problem has happened.
- We apologise for . . .

After you have got into the main part of the letter, the range of language that you may wish to express is very wide. Below is a list of some typical functions that you may need. After each is the reference to the relevant unit in section A.

1. Connecting ideas – Unit 35, and Connecting and sequencing ideas – Unit 67
2. Agreeing and disagreeing – Unit 76
3. Advising and suggesting – Unit 81
4. Requesting information and action – Unit 82
5. Comparing and contrasting ideas – Unit 72
6. Asserting and toning down information – Unit 70
7. Asking for and giving opinions – Unit 75

SKILL 5
Report-writing

Background

Peter Drucker has written: 'Effective communication has four parts – something we have known since Plato and Aristotle – only our businessmen never seem to have heard of the task. One has to know:

> what to say
> when to say it
> to whom to say it
> how to say it

If one of those elements is missing, there cannot be communication.' (*Communicate*, Parkinson, C. M. and Rowe, N., Prentice Hall, 1978). This is as true for report-writing as for other forms of management communication – both oral and written.

So, what exactly is a report? It is:

> a written statement
> prepared for the benefit of others
> describing what has happened or a state of affairs
> normally based on investigation

So, what are the elements of an effective report?

1. The effective organisation of the information.
2. The effective presentation of the information.
3. The effective style of delivery.
4. The effective use of language.

And, before you start . . .

5. Decide why you are writing the report (the purpose).
6. Plan the content and the structure (the planning stage).
7. And finally never forget your readers.

Now let's expand points 1–4 to identify the skills and techniques you need.

1. Organisation of information

    a. Transparency of structure (from title page to appendices)
    b. Organisation of content (identify clearly main points and supporting points)
    c. Level of information (start in the readers' area of interest)

2. Presentation of information

    a. Ease of reading (layout, headings and indentations; use of spaces; use of paragraphs)
    b. Ease of understanding (language and visuals)

3. Style of delivery

    a. Clarity (content and follow-up)
    b. Simplicity (appropriate to the readers' level of knowledge)
    c. Conciseness (appropriate length)
    d. Company style
    e. Personal tone

4. Use of language

    a. Vocabulary (choose the right word in written language rather than spoken language)
    b. Grammar (assemble the sentences correctly in terms of language forms)
    c. Phraseology (choose appropriate expressions for the business/technical area)
    d. Spelling (make sure it is correct and consistent – either Br.E. or Am.E.)
    e. Linking and punctuation (use them to help readers with the relationships between ideas and the structure of the text)
    f. Fog Index (do not exceed 12 – see below)

Checklist of operations

1. Plan your report
2. Collect the information
3. Select the information
4. Organise the information
5. Produce a plan and visuals
6. Write the first draft
7. Read the first draft and check for tone and content
8. Write a summary
9. Write final draft

Planning your report

1. Think about your objectives

    a. What is the change you wish to bring about in your readers?
    b. Do you want to inform them, change their ideas, elicit ideas or amuse them? Or a combination of these?

2. Think about the audience

    a. What type of people are they?
    b. What is their present level of knowledge on the subject?
    c. What do you want them to know after they have read the report?
    d. What is their level of understanding of English?

3. Think about the time

    a. How much time do you need in order to prepare your report?
    b. How much time do the readers have in order to read your report?
    c. Then balance the equation

4. *Think about the information*

    a.   How much in essential?
    b.   What is the best length of individual items?

5. *Think about the structure and presentation*

    a.   What is the best way to organise and present the report so that it achieves your objectives?

Structuring your report

The standard pattern

If you are writing a formal report, the standard pattern is:

1. Title page
2. Table of contents*
3. Summary or abstract*
4. Introduction
5. The main part of the report
6. Conclusions
7. Recommendations
8. Appendices*
9. Bibliography or references*
10. Exhibits

You can leave out those marked with an arterisk (*) if you don't need them.

Although the above pattern is standard, it is not universal. Some people like to put the conclusions and recommendations before the introduction; others like to put the summary, conclusions and recommendations after the introduction.

There are two possible numbering systems: traditional and decimal.

Traditional

    First level: use cardinal numbers – 1, 2, 3, etc.
    Second level: use letters in brackets – (a), (b), (c), etc.
    Third level: use Roman numerals in brackets – (i), (ii), (iii), etc.

Decimal

All levels: use cardinal numbers, separated by decimal points, e.g.

    First level: 1, 2, 3, etc.
    Second level: 1.1, 1.2, 1.3, etc.
    Third level: 1.1.1, 1.1.2, 1.1.3, etc.

Do not use more than three levels in either system, as it is confusing.

The purpose and content of each of the sections 1–9 above is shown now in more detail:

1. The *title page*. This should give:

    > the subject of the report
    > by whom the report is made
    > the date of the report
    > the file, serial or reference number

    All this should be clearly laid out. Uniformity in the style of cover and title pages is an advantage and the standard pattern of the area or department should be used.

2. The *table of contents*. As in a book, this lists all the headings in the report and the pages or, in short reports, the paragraphs. It should show the relationship of headings and subheadings by indentation or by different types or size of print.

3. *Summary or abstract.* This gives the substance of the report in a nutshell – mainly the important conclusions. It should serve to catch the interest and focus the attention of those to whom the report is addressed. It can enable others, who may be interested, to decide whether they wish to read the report.

4. The *Introduction* (or terms of reference and methods and procedures). This tells the reader why the report was written (including a clear statement of the problem or problems to be considered), who asked for it, who did the investigation, who wrote the report, what the scope and limitations of the investigation and report are, where the information was obtained, any special methods used and acknowledgements of help given. It sets the scene before the reader gets down to the body of the report.

5. The *main part of the report*. This gives the facts, discusses them and makes certain deductions about them. If it is a large subject, the facts may be split up under a number of sub-headings and discussed in turn. After the facts and the deductions comes an examination of possible courses of action with an accurate assessment of the advantages and disadvantages of each. Such things as cost, manpower and equipment will need to be taken into account and discussed. The continuity of the report should not be interrupted by material which could go into an appendix.

6. *Conclusions.* These are the conclusions based on the evidence and alternatives given in the previous part of the report. Sometimes this section is only a reiteration of conclusions stated at the end of each subsection of the main body of the report. No new material should appear in the conclusions. Everything must flow logically from the facts and discussion and alternatives shown in the previous part of the report. Conclusions should be clear and concise. Remember that some people will read only the introduction, conclusions and recommendations so they must be intelligible and in a logical order.

7. *Recommendations.* These state the action which the writer of the report advises on the strength of the evidence, discussion and conclusions. The recommendations made should be developed from the views expressed in the main part of the report. A person who chooses to read only the introduction, conclusions and recommendations ought to be able to go back to the main part of the report and see the evidence for these. Recommendations which have no roots in the main part of the report should not appear. Each recommendation must be given a letter or number.

8. *Appendices.* Information which is for reference rather than part of the argument should be put in an appendix. Appendices should be grouped together at the end of the report and set out so that they can be read the same way up as the rest of the report. Even if the paper has to be folded, it is better than expecting the reader to turn the report sideways to refer to an appendix. Each appendix should bear a title. It should be marked Appendix
A, Appendix B and so on or Appendix I, II, III in the top right-hand corner. Refer in the text to each appendix and state what is significant about it.

9. *Bibliography.* This consists of lists of books, reports, etc., which have been used. The interested reader may want to read more about the subject.

10. *Exhibits.* These are large sheets and diagrams. These should be folded and put in plastic envelopes if they cannot be bound into the report.

Writing your report

The language

> Prefer the **familiar** word to the far-fetched.
> Prefer the **concrete** word to the abstract.
> Prefer the **single** word to the circumlocution.
> Prefer the **short** word to the long.
> Prefer the **Saxon** word to the Romance.
>   – Fowler

The range of language appropriate to reports is very wide. You can find many of the key language areas in section A part 1 – Grammar – and in section A part 2 – Functions.
 Below are some units that you may wish to refer to:

1. Verbs of reporting – Unit 25
2. Connecting ideas – Unit 35
3. Reported speech – Unit 37
4. Classifying information – Unit 66
5. Describing trends – Unit 68
6. Comparing and contrasting ideas – Unit 72
7. Cause and effect – Unit 77
8. Obligations and requirements – Unit 78
9. Scale of likelihood – Unit 80

The Fog Index

After you have drafted your report, make sure you check it thoroughly. Check the total report for fluency, logic and comprehensibility; check all sentences for clarity and length. Remember, longer sentences are usually harder to understand than shorter ones. One way to measure the readability of your report is to use Robert Gunning's 'Fog Index'. This is a mathematical guide based on sentence length. You calculate the index as follows:

$$F = 0.4 \, (A + L)$$

where F = Fog Index

A = Average length of sentences (a full stop, colon or semi-colon equals the end of a sentence)

L = Number of long words per hundred words of text. A long word has three or more syllables, but excludes the following endings: **-ed**, **-es**, or **-ing**.

The resulting index shows the number of years of education needed to understand the text. In the UK, education starts at the age of five. Therefore, when writing for the general public, writers should aim for a Fog Index of 10; when writing for a professional public, an index of 14–15 is acceptable, though 12 is preferable.

SKILL 6
Social language

Background

Social language is as much a part of professional communication as presentation and report-writing skills. In fact, perhaps even more business is conducted outside the boardroom than in it. So what exactly are social language skills? They are the skills which enable people to be comfortable with each other without a formal agenda – when meeting, when making small talk, when discussing matters of mutual interest and when parting. Of course, not every native speaker has this skill. But, nevertheless, a lot can be done to prepare the non-native speaker for the types of situation and the varieties of language that he or she may encounter.

So, what makes an effective socialiser?

1. The ability to behave appropriately in different cross-cultural situations.
2. The ability to start conversations.
3. The ability to reply appropriately.
4. The ability to select safe topics for conversation.
5. The ability to develop conversations around different topics.

Making friends and influencing people

Here are some tips for behaviour either when you are in the UK or together with Britons.

1. Starters

  a. Not everybody shakes hands on meeting or parting
  b. If you do, shake hands firmly but not too long
  c. Look your opposite number straight in the eye
  d. Smile
  e. Always make sure you hear the name
  f. If you don't, ask for a repetition
  g. If it is still difficult, ask for the spelling
  h. Use the name for a while

2. Making contact

  a. Start with safe areas
  b. Acknowledge what you hear
  c. Comment or ask questions to keep the conversation going
  d. If you don't hear or understand, ask for a repetition
  e. If in doubt, smile – don't frown

3. Developing contact

  a. Keep to safe topic areas until you are sure that you will not cause offence
  b. Do not monopolise the conversation

   c. Make comments and ask for opinions
   d. If in difficulty, remember people usually like to talk about themselves.

4. Moving on

   a. Decide when to finish the conversation or leave
   b. Be firm and clear
   c. Give a reason
   d. Smile before and as you go

Now, let's take a look at some key situations of social contact and the language you can use.

Social contact

Greetings and introductions

Often the greetings and the introductions follow this sequence:

greeting
introducing oneself or someone else
reply to introduction

1. Greeting and introducing oneself at the first meeting

Greeting	Introducing oneself	Reply
How do you do?	I'm . . .	How do you do? I'm . . .
Pleased to meet you	My name is . . .	Pleased to meet you, too Mine's . . .
Nice to meet you Glad to meet you		Nice to meet you, too Glad to meet you, too

'How do you do?' is not really a question: it is not a request for information.

2. Greeting someone at the second and subsequent meetings

Greeting	Reply
How are you?	Very well, thanks. And you? Fine, thanks. And you? Not too bad/So-so/Could be worse Not too good, I'm afraid Absolutely awful/terrible/dreadful

This greeting often comes after the following exchange:

- A: Nice to see you.
  B: Nice to see you, too.

a. The greeting 'How are you?' is a real question and request for information.
b. There is usually a difference between 'meet' for a first meeting and 'see' for a second and subsequent meeting, e.g. 'Pleased to meet you' (first time), 'Nice to see you' (subsequent time).
c. After 'Not too good, I'm afraid' and 'Absolutely awful/terrible/dreadful', it is common and polite for the other person to ask, 'What's the matter/problem?'

3. **Introducing oneself and getting on first-name terms**

- My name is . . . | Please call me . . .
                    | You can call me . . .

4. **Introducing someone else**

- May I introduce. . . ?
- I'd like to introduce . . .
- This is . . .

5. **Acknowledging information**
   When we exchange information in a conversation, we have three strategies that we can use to indicate that we understand and to encourage the speaker to continue:

Noises	Words/phrases	Echo
Uh-huh	Okay	Sixty thousand?
Mm	Right	Six hundred years?
Ah	Fine	The biggest in Europe?
Oh	Really?	
	Amazing!	
	I see	
	I know	
	Yes	
	No	
	I didn't know that	
	I can't believe that	
	Quite (so)	
	Indeed	
	Of course	

Presenting yourself

Here are some typical areas that you can use to identify yourself, together with some appropriate language:

1. **Work**

What do you do?

I work as a factory manager. (job title)
I work for an electronics company. (company sector)
I'm retired.

Who do you work for?

I work for Ebor Electronics. (name of employer)
Actually, I'm self-employed

What do they do?	We/They make electronic components. (activity)
Where are you based?	We are based in York. (location)
And what exactly do you do?	I'm responsible for the quality control of silicon chips.
How many people do you employ?	Oh, I suppose about five hundred in the UK.
How long have you been there?	Five years now.
Do you think you will stay?	Well, that's a difficult question. It all depends.

2. Home

So, where do you live?	Just outside York.
Whereabouts is that?	That's in the northeast of England.
Do you live in a house or a flat?	In a house.
What's it like?	Fairly modern, with four bedrooms.

3. Origins and family

And are you from here originally?	No, actually I was born in Manchester. I moved here about fifteen years ago.
Do you have any family?	Yes, I'm married with two children: a girl and a boy.
How old are they?	The boy's seven and the girl's four.
And does your wife work?	Not at the moment. She's at home with our daughter.
And your son?	Oh, he's at school.

Here and there

Here are some safe topics for the next stage, as you explore what you have in common:

1. Here

Is this your first visit to the UK?	No, I come here quite often.
Have you been in York before?	No, actually this is my first visit.
Business or pleasure?	Business, I'm afraid.
How long have you been here?	Just over two days.
When did you arrive?	Late Sunday night.
How long are you staying?	Till tomorrow.
Where are you staying?	At the Viking hotel.
Is it comfortable?	Yes, very.
What's the food like?	Fine.
So, what do you think of York?	Lovely, it's really old and interesting.
So, what are you doing this evening?	I was thinking of having a quiet evening.

2. Weather

So, how was the weather in Oslo?	Oh, much the same as here.
What was the weather like in . . . ?	Much warmer than here.
Isn't this weather terrible/wonderful?	Absolutely awful/fabulous!
Is the weather always like this?	No, this is exceptional.

3. **Travel**
Have you ever been to South America?
Have you ever visited Rio de Janeiro?
Where are you travelling to?
Where are you off to next?

4. **Interests**

So, what do you do in your spare time?	Oh, I play a little golf.
Is . . . popular in your country?	Quite popular.
Is it expensive?	Not if you join a club.
Are you interested in sport?	Yes, I like watching tennis.
Do you play?	I used to.

5. **The world**
Do you use English in your job?
I see inflation is rising here.
How is the unemployment situation in your country?
Is drink a problem in your country?
What sort of government do you have?

Safe and unsafe topics of conversation

The range of acceptable topics of conversation will depend on:

> where you are
> who you are with
> your relationship with the people

Here is a list of **safe topics** for conversation with Britons:

> House and home
> Life at home
> Education and career
> Work
> Free time and entertainment
> Travel
> Health and welfare
> Shopping
> Food and drink
> Services
> Geography of the UK and places to visit
> Weather
> The economy
> Politics

Here is a list of topics which may be **dangerous**:

> Family relationships
> The Royal Family
> Trade unions
> The situation in Northern Ireland
> The British affection for pets

Now here are some **do's** and **don'ts**:

Do

> Be punctual for social meetings
> Bring a small gift if you are invited to someone's home
> Use 'please' and 'thank you' for requests and services

Don't

> Make too much physical contact
> Be aggressive and loud
> Be over-enthusiastic
> Ask too many personal questions
> Call the Welsh, Scots and Irish 'English'

Hospitality

As we have noted above, a lot of business is done over meals and drinks. So, the professional needs to be able to handle a range of social situations in restaurants and bars.

1. **Making an invitation**
Would you like to join us for dinner this evening?
How about a drink in the bar before dinner?
We would like to invite you for dinner tomorrow evening?

2. **Accepting an invitation**
Thank you, I'd love to/be delighted.
Thank you, that sounds very nice.
An excellent idea.

3. **Declining an invitation**
I'm afraid I need an early night – I'll have to say no.
I'm afraid I can't make it tonight.
I'd love to, but I've got another engagement.
I'm sorry, but I've got to leave very early tomorrow morning.

4. **In the bar**

How/What about a drink?	Good idea.
Would you like a drink?	That would be nice.
	Yes, please
	No, thanks/thank you.
	I'd love to but I'm driving.
	I'm afraid I can't.
What can I get you?	I'd like a gin and tonic.
What would you like to drink?	Could I have a whiskey, please?
	I'll have a dry sherry, please.
	Mine's a pint of bitter.

(*Offering to pay*)
Let me get this one/these.
This/these is/are on me.
This is my round.

(*Moving into the restaurant*)
Right, shall we go into the restaurant now?   Yes, let's.
Right, let's go into the restaurant now, shall we?   Yes, let's.

5. **In the restaurant**

a. *Ordering*
What would you like as a starter/main course/desert?
Would you like meat or fish?
Would you like to try one of our specialities?
What would you recommend?
I'd recommend the fish. It's usually excellent here.
And what would you like to drink?

b. *Eating*
Bon appetit! (Some people use the French expression as there is no English expression)
How is your soup/salad/meat/fish?
It's delicious.
I'm afraid it's cold/too salty/over-cooked
Can I order/get you something else?
Would you like | another glass of wine?   Yes, please.
               | some more wine?   No, thanks.

c. *Digesting*
Would you like a coffee/liqueur?
Well, that was really excellent!

d. *Preparing to leave*
Well, I really must make a move.
Well, I really must get back to my hotel.
I'm afraid I'll have to leave now.
I'm sorry to break up the party, but I have to make a very early start tomorrow morning.
Do you think you could order a taxi for me?

e. *Thanking*
I'd like to thank you for a most enjoyable   It's been a pleasure.
evening.

Polite responses

Knowing the right polite response can make everyone feel more comfortable. Here is a list of things to say and to reply in a variety of situations.

1. **When someone thanks you**	**You respond . . .**
Thanks for the present	Not at all
Thanks for a lovely evening	Don't mention it
	My pleasure
	Glad you enjoyed it

2. **When someone apologises**	**You respond**
Oh, I'm so sorry. I seem to have lost his address	
	Never mind
	It doesn't matter
	Don't worry
	Not to worry

3. When someone asks your permission

May I come in?	Yes, of course
	Please do
Can I ask you a question?	Certainly
	Go ahead
Do you mind if I smoke?	(*Refusing permission*)
	Well, actually I'd rather you didn't (*polite*)
	Yes, I do actually (*direct*)
	(*Giving permission*)
	No, not at all
	Of course not

4. When you give something to someone

Could you pass me the . . ., please?	Of course. Here you are
Have you got the tickets?	Yes, here they are
	Here are your tickets

5. When you haven't heard properly

	Sorry?
	(I beg your) pardon?
	I didn't quite catch that/what you said
	Could you repeat that, please?

6. To express comfort

I didn't get that job	Well, never mind
	Well, better luck next time

7. To express sympathy

We missed the plane	Oh, hard/bad luck!
My aunt died last night	Oh, I am sorry (to hear that)

8. To express surprise

He's the managing director	Really!

9. **To express agreement and**
   disagreement with an opinion

   You respond

I think the food is overpriced

(*Agreement*)
Very true
Quite
Exactly
(*Disagreement*)
Do you (really) think so?
I don't think so
Surely not

10. **To express agreement and disagreement with a fact**

Of course, they are very efficient

(*Agreement*)
Very true
Yes, you're quite right
Yes, that's true
(*Disagreement*)
Do you (really) think so?
No, it isn't
Are you sure?
Surely not

11. **To confirm information**

In France you normally have the cheese
before the dessert, don't you?

Yes, that's right
No, that's not quite right

12. **When someone makes a request**

Could you take this through customs for me?

(*Accepting*)
Yes, of course (I will)
Yes, certainly
(*Refusing*)
I'd rather not, if you don't mind (*polite*)
No, I can't do that (*direct*)
Certainly not (*abrupt*)

13. **To express apology**

Excuse me. Could you tell me how to get to the station? (*getting attention*)
Excuse me. Could you let me through? (*apologising before the event*)
Excuse me/Sorry. Can I just come in here? (*interrupting a conversation*)
I'm very/terribly sorry. (*apologising after the event*)
Sorry (*apologising after the event*)
Sorry? (*Br.E. – asking for repetition because you haven't heard or understood*)
Excuse me? (*Am.E. – asking for repetition because you haven't heard or understood*)

14. **To wish someone luck**

All the best!
The best of luck!

Thanks!

Parting

Well, (it's been) nice meeting you. (It's been) nice to have met you.	Likewise
I think we've had a very fruitful meeting.	Yes, me too
I look forward to seeing you in Madrid. See you again.	Likewise Bye
Have a good trip. All the best.	The same to you.

You can find more language for social contact in the following units in section A part 2 – Functions.

1. Describing the organisation – Unit 69
2. Asserting and toning down information – Unit 70
3. Checking and confirming information – Unit 73
4. Likes and preferences – Unit 74
5. Asking for and giving opinions – Unit 75
6. Agreeing and disagreeing – Unit 76
7. Advising and suggesting – Unit 81
8. Requesting information and action – Unit 82

Checklist for effective communication

- **With whom** am I going to communicate?
- What are my **objectives** in doing so?
- What is likely to be the **receiver's view of the subject matter** of the communication?
- What is likely to be the **receiver's view of me?** (i.e. what are the likely **barriers** to effective communication?)
- **Who else** do I need to involve, inform, get ideas and information from?
- What is likely to be the **most effective medium** and **channel** of communication in order to achieve my objectives?

Index